UnDOING
CHURCH
DISCOVERING
FAITH

KATHY PRIDE

UnDoing Church
Discovering Faith

ISBN: 978-1-936417-52-0
RELIGION / CHRISTIAN LIFE / DEVOTIONAL

Published by h2press

HOW TO REACH KATHY PRIDE:
www.undoingchurch.com

"Unlearning is more important and more difficult than learning. This study will help you unlearn and rethink you faith from the ground up. Get ready for a paradigm shift.
— Mark Batterson, Author, Pastor Theater Church

Everywhere I go, followers of Jesus are trying to figure out what the church should be in a world plagued by global warming, overpopulation, and economic and political upheaval, but very few of them are taking the time to let God speak to them on the subject through the Bible. I applaud Kathy Pride for devising a guide for doing just that, and pray that many will find their answers — and new missions for their lives — in this way."
— Bart Campolo, Author, Speaker, President of EAP

"Actually I think my Momma would dig this Bible study...she's pretty sassy (now my granny would be a different story). But this is not for folks who are satisfied with the fluffy devotionals that line the shelves of so many Christian retail stores. This book is for the over-churched and the no-churched. It is for the under-nourished souls that know there is more to Christianity than what's on TV. It is a book for the growing movement of soccer moms, subversive nannies, and empty-nest dreamers who are ready to live their faith with creativity and courage, and with the Kingdom hope that another world is possible."
— Shane Claiborne, Recovering Sinner, Activist, and Author of *The Irresistible Revolution* and *Jesus for President*.

"Reading what Kathy writes in not like reading a normal book. It really does feel like you are actually sitting there with her, drinking a coffee and getting some really wonderful and soulful insight from what she shares."
— Dan Kimball, Pastor of Vintage Faith Church and author of *They Like Jesus but not the Church*

"Kathy Pride gives women permission to be real and authentic as they strive towards womanhood in a Biblical and practical manner."
— Dr. David A. Anderson, Author of *Gracism*, Pastor Bridgeway Community Church

"Reading Kathy Prides' Bible study, you get the impression that she's not trying to solicit the 'Sunday School' response. She is honest, and in return, the study evokes honest communication, with oneself, with fellow study participants, and with God. For those who have grown up in the church it is a wakeup call: those around us don't need our pretense, our perfection, or our 'Christianese' — they need our Christ."
— Peter Greer, President, HOPE International

"If you've ever felt bewildered, bored or frustrated by church of Bible Study, Kathy Pride will be like a ray of hope. *Undoing Church* is a straight forward, refreshing look at what it means to be a follower of Christ in today's world. This is definitely not your mother's Bible study!"
— Jud Wilhite, Senior Pastor of Central Christian Church, Las Vegas, Author, *Stripped: Uncensored Grace in Sin City*

"Kathy knocks the ball right out of the pews—and perhaps through the steeple-with this entertaining and provocative study! Without being an iconoclast, Kathy dials in the pulse of our unchurched culture and then amplifies it with humor and compassion. As a former pastor and one who now helps pastors and churches reinvent themselves, I find myself inspired toward greater honesty and creativity by Kathy's no-nonsense approach. Turn this book loose in your life, in your neighborhood and in your church if you dare."
— Jerome Daley, Leadership Coach and Church Consultant, Editor of the *Journal of Christian Coaching*, author of *The New Rebellion Handbook*

"Kathy has done a great job creating a Bible Study for people using language and examples that make it 'really normal.' When reviewing materials for our groups, we use great caution to make sure the language is consistent with our culture of ministry. Finding a Bible Study that is a fit for those who are new to Christianity or who are returning is not easy. This is a great Bible Study for anyone!"
— Kathy Guy, Director of Community, Granger Community Church

"In our culture, it's difficult to find consistency in our time with God and study of the Scripture. Kathy captures timeless Biblical wisdom and makes it easy to find that path to consistency in her Bible Study, *Undoing Church*. You'll be challenged and excited to see what's next, each and every day."
— Anne Jackson, Christian Blogger, Author of *Mad Church Disease*

"*Undoing Church* invites all women whether they grace a pew on Sunday mornings or not to explore the difference between following Christ and following a prescribed set of religious rules. In her transparent style, Kathy invites you into a conversation that is guaranteed to challenge and edify."
— Tammy Maltby, Aspiring Women TV host, Author, *Confessions of a Good Christian Girl*

"I'm always on the hunt for resources that aren't same-o, same-o. Kathy Pride brings fresh expressions of faith that push back on musty stereotypes which hinder many from deeper connection with God. *UnDoing Church* provides a fresh take on knowing Jesus without disrespecting our traditions that often limit us. I like any resource able to do that."
— Alan Nelson, Former Editor *Rev! Magazine*, Founder KidSpeak

"In *UnDoing Church*, Kathy Pride invites us to find previously UnSeen resources in the Scriptures to help us UnLearn and ReLearn, so we can UnLock deeper transformation and UnLeash more of our God-given potential."
— Brian McLaren, Author/Speaker

"I've been reading Christian books for 33 years. I know there is no shortage of Christian books or Bible Studies. But Kathy Pride has made a truly unique contribution. Christianity is in an awkward relationship with the wider culture at this point in time. Most Christians — and seekers alike — have lost confidence in how to feel, act and think "right." Pride illumines a way forward with mature clarity, non-judgmental joy and good humor. I highly commend *UnDoing Church*.
— Todd Hunter, Church Planter, The Anglican Mission in the Americas, Past President Alpha USA, Past President Vineyard Churches, USA

"Kathy Pride has written a study that will cause you to see scripture with fresh eyes. At times I bet you'll cringe. At times I know you'll ponder and mull over what she points out. But just as often, you'll feel that rush of liberation that comes whenever we realize that we're not alone-that others have seen and wondered the same things we have-and actually have the courage to say it out loud."
— Larry Osborne, Author and Pastor, North Coast Church

"Every generation needs to understand the timeless gospel in a timely way. Kathy has written an engaging study to help a new generation understand the absolute adventure of following Jesus."
— Eric Swanson, Author, *The Externally Focused Church*

"Certain authors write chicken soup for the soul. More to my taste are less soupy, more saucy authors like Kathy Pride — who write hot sauce for the spirit, and juice your brain with mind-expanding, soul-stretching visions and voices. I'm hooked for life."
— Leonard Sweet, Drew University, George Fox Evangelical Seminary

"Getting to know...really know people who do not attend church is the first step toward engaging in dialogue and ultimately explaining the claims of Christ. Kathy Pride offers a simple, straightforward and engaging Bible Study that will help women begin a dialogue with those who do not attend church. This bible study can help all Christians understand what others think, how to authentically inaugurate a dialogue and ultimately how to introduce them to a best new friend: Jesus Christ."
— Bob Whitesel, D.Min. Ph.D., author of *Preparing for Change Reaction, How to Introduce Change in Your Church* and associate professor in the College of Graduate Studies at Indiana Wesleyan University.

*i*NTRODU*C*T*i*ON

Christians have a responsibility to share their faith, in fact, the Bible commands us to.

This project was born of a dream to do just that in a way I wish someone had with me.

Perhaps I would have engaged in conversations about Jesus earlier, but too many Christians had turned me off. Many of the Christians I had met or known were pretty judgmental and hypocritical individuals; there was a huge disconnect between what they said they believed and how they behaved.

My vision for this project included a cover that would generate a response, identical to the one you now see. However, early in the development of this title there was controversy over putting such a provoking image on the cover. I held on to the vision God gave me for generating discussion about the church and faith and welcome you to church, the people, not the building.

CONTENTS:

week one:

But I Always Thought Church Was Just a Building

Okay, here's the deal. There was a time when I thought church was simply a building. You know: "Here is the church and here is the steeple." Four walls that created a building where people go on Sunday mornings to do I wasn't sure what—fulfill a commitment, absolve themselves of guilt, sing a few hymns, have a reason to get dressed up. Whatever.

But worship God? That wasn't part of the equation as far as I *was* concerned. It was a building. Period.

For most of my life I was under the impression church was a place, or a destination on a city tour; St. Patrick's Cathedral if you were visiting New York City, Notre Dame if you happened to be sojourning in Paris.

When I was a child my experience with church was limited. Once a year my family attended Christmas Eve service at Riverside Church on the upper west side of New York City, where we sang familiar Christmas carols and there were lots of pretty candles. My other experiences were limited to the mandatory attendance at church on Sunday mornings when I went to visit my Grandma Knauf in upstate New York.

I remember periodically asking my parents why we didn't go to church, and getting some vague answers about Sunday being a day to relax and our lives being too full.

Until I was well into middle age (how I hate that term) the connection between church (it was a building) and worship (praise and fellowship with God?) was nonexistent for me.

The notion that church is NOT a place, but rather a collection of those who are Christians, or Christ-followers, was a long time in coming. It took more than a little getting used to.

What did you just say, Kathy? you're asking. *Church is not just a building? And going to church is not just a Sunday date? You're kidding, right? And worship isn't about me—it's about praising God? I can only absorb so much new information at one time, and this is a stretch. Not to mention that I can't understand what those church people are talking about most of the time anyway. They use words and phrases I have never heard before, and half the time I end up feeling judged and somehow like I don't get it.*

Yeah, I know—it took some getting used to for me, too. But church is so much more than a building. It isn't a place. It is the collective followers of a *person*. And that person is Jesus Christ.

Welcome to church.

DAY ONE:

CHURCH DOESN'T ALWAYS HAVE FOUR WALLS

THOUGHT FOR THE DAY

Remember: The church is the followers of Christ, not the building or place of worship.

WHAT DO YOU BELIEVE?

1. What impressions of church did you develop as a child?
2. Did you grow up believing church was a building that had to look a certain way?
3. Did you go to church as a child?
4. If so, did you go with your family or with someone else?

WHAT OTHERS MAY THINK

Church is:

a. The place to which you drag your kids kicking and screaming on Sunday mornings because that is what "good" families do.

b. The really, really pretty building with stained-glass windows you go to twice a year (Christmas and Easter, in case you weren't sure), which is your ticket to heaven.

c. The place where the ladies with blue hair and too many pearls go on Sunday mornings so they can catch up on a week's worth of gossip.
d. Those of us who serve as Christ's hands and feet here on Earth. Through service we demonstrate we are part of the body of Christ—his committed followers worldwide.

I remember vividly the day I went to church, for real, for the first time—the first time I sensed that church was more than four walls. It was a gathering place for the followers of Jesus, committed to serving him as part of his body. For the first time I experienced the true definition of *church*: a group of people who served as his hands and feet here on Earth.

It was an Aha! moment. And I was in my forties.

Have you had an experience like that? Describe it:

Have you had an experience with just two or three others when you've been aware of God's presence?

Did you ever think of that as "church"?

Who was with you? (Who were the two or three?)

Where were you? Describe the place and what it was that connected you to God.

I recall my pastor asking me shortly after I accepted Christ as my Savior (what on earth did that mean, anyway?), "How long has God been calling your name?" When I stopped to think about it, I realized it had been since I was a teenager.

I remembered a time long ago when I was in Switzerland. I was standing on the balcony of a chalet built around 1790, in a hamlet of a town seemingly untouched by time (except for the satellite dishes).

I stared out into space at the black velvet sky, punctuated by glistening stars that beckoned me to a reality far beyond what I could see. That was when I first sensed a power greater than myself, the first time I felt God wooing me, although I didn't understand or recognize it at the time. It was not until several years later that I realized God was inviting me into a relationship with him.

Isn't that always the way? Hindsight is 20/20.

Describe a time in your life when hindsight revealed that God may have been wooing you. What stands out to you about that memory? What allows you to believe it was God trying to start a conversation with you?

Do you think you need to be within the four walls of a church building to hear and speak with God?

A NEW WAY TO BELIEVE

Look up the following verses. Do any of them stretch your definition of church?

Matthew 18:20

Matthew 16:18

Matthew 18:17

Acts 20:28

1 Corinthians 14:12

1 Corinthians 14:26

Colossians 1:24

Which verse most closely relates to how you view church and your role as a part of the church?

If you could describe the ideal church, what would it look like?

Now translate those attributes to yourself. Should you be displaying them to those around you?

Not long ago I had the opportunity to join a women's ministry meal with a friend in California. It was so refreshing! The meeting was in a warehouse annex converted into a coffee shop, where overstuffed chairs surrounded bistro tables, complete with the opportunity to order lattes for us java junkies. Church services were held in the warehouse.

That stretched my concept of "church." Yet it was the perfect place to sit down, kick back, and enter into honest dialog about life past, present, and future.

Is there an "unconventional" but welcoming place (that you might not have thought of up 'til now) where you can introduce the love of Christ to others? Make it your goal this week to find such a place.

List three places where you could be "the church" to others:
1.
2.
3.

BELIEVE AND ACT
· You don't need a building to worship God.
· List three places you can worship God.
· Christ is with you everywhere.
· Bring church into your home.

ASK THROUGH PRAYER
Thank you, Jesus, for your body, which is the church. Thank you for helping me see my place and role as part of the body of Christ, your church. Thank you that wherever two or three are gathered, there we find you. Amen.

Worship: Not Just a Pretty Song

THOUGHT FOR THE DAY

As you refocus your thinking about church as God's people rather than a building, it is also necessary to stretch and redefine how you think about worship. It is more than a song. It is every way you communicate love to God.

WHAT DO YOU BELIEVE?

1. When you think of worship, what comes to mind?
2. Do you go to church to worship God, or to get something out of it for yourself?
3. Can performing your job be an act of worship?
4. Is it more meaningful to God if you worship him at church on Sunday morning than if you worship him alone in your car on Thursday afternoon?

WHAT OTHERS MAY THINK

Worship is:

a. What your older sister says you better do to the ground she walks on if you ever want to borrow anything from her ever, ever again.

b. The singing in church.

c. How we feel about our new house, new car, new
   wardrobe, or any other newly acquired possession until
   it is replaced by the upgraded model.

d. How we express our love to God.

I was in for a rude surprise. Church, and going to church, was not about me, or pleasing my parents or grandparents, for that matter. Oh, or to avoid some vague sense of guilt because it was the "thing to do." Rather, it was about my worship for God and what I could do for him.

Which of the following describe what you think about going to church?

· I should because it is expected, either by someone else or
  the nagging little voice inside my head.
· I can socialize with the people.
· There is a meal served the third Sunday of every month
  after service and the food is awesome, especially the
  desserts.
· If I go to church, I will go to heaven.
· I can worship God in a group setting during a time specifically set aside to let God know how much I love him,
  and learn how to serve him better and how to get to
  know him better.

While the first four reasons may certainly be fringe benefits of going to church, the driving force behind attending church is to worship God.

And to think I bought into the misguided notions. After all, church is the place you go on Sunday mornings to catch up with a certain group of friends, get your spiritual cup filled, and climb another step closer to heaven, right? Wrong.

Church is the place you go *to worship God.*

Now just one more. Before I could really give my full attention to God, I had to get rid of those pesky distractions that keep popping up like those frogs at the arcade in the lily pad game.

You know the one: the game where you have a bopper and frogs pop up all over the place and you have to eliminate them before they disap-pear back under the lily pad. Before you can wholeheartedly give your heart to God you need to think about the other things you worship in your life:

· Power
· Your job
· Soap operas
· Money
· Jewelry
· Nice clothes (I especially like clothing from Chico's.)
· My collection of . . .
· My family

Don't get me wrong—it is fine to work, earn a living, dress nicely, and spend time with your family, but not at the expense of spending time with God.

Think about these words, spoken by Jonah: *"Those who cling to worthless idols forfeit the grace that could be theirs"* (Jonah 2:8).

Are you clinging to worthless idols, and if so, what?

Write a prayer expressing any need you may have for help:

A NEW WAY TO BELIEVE

Look up the following verses. What do these verses say about worship? What kinds of acts are described in these verses that are ways to worship God?

Deuteronomy 8:10

Deuteronomy 11:1

Psalm 27:6

Psalm 29:2

Psalm 145:10

John 9:31

John 4:23-24

Which of the following do you believe describe acts of worship?

· Praise
· Prayer
· Rejoicing
· Silent meditation
· Singing in church
· Singing in the car
· Listening to Christian music
· Performing a random act of kindness
· Doing your job to the best of your ability
· Giving 110 percent effort on the playing field
· Handing in homework or a job assignment in its neatest
   possible form

Do you think the way you use your body can be an act of worship? Put an "X" where you fall:

__ Never
__ Rarely

___ Sometimes
___ Usually
___ Most of the time
___ Always

Read Romans 12:1. How can our body be a living sacrifice and spiritual act of worship?

List ways you can use each of the following body parts as a way to worship God:

· Eyes

· Ears

· Mouth

What does Psalm 95:6 say about posture for worship?

Why do you think kneeling is an important posture? (Trivia: There are more than 100 references in the Bible to kneeling in worship).

And, as Psalm 63:4 says, "I will praise you as long as I live, and in your name I will lift up my hands." I think it is safe to say lifting our hands to God is yet another example of how we can use our bodies in worship.

Convinced yet? While worship may involve singing, it is more than a song!

BELIEVE AND ACT
· You can worship while you are at home, at your job, in the
car, or at church.

· You can worship by singing, dancing, and using your hands
  and feet!
· God will gladly accept your worship 24/7.

ASK THROUGH PRAYER

Father God, help me worship you and not the stuff in my life, of which there is just way too much. Help me focus more on you and less on the stuff, and experience the joy that only worshipping you can provide.

Amen.

Day Three:

Is Church Just a Sunday Date?

THOUGHT FOR THE DAY

As we continue to focus on the concept that church is not a place but the followers of Christ, and worship is a way to honor him, let's think about how we have traditionally viewed church: as the place we go on Sunday morning.

WHAT DO YOU BELIEVE?

1. When you think about going to church on Sunday, are you excited or apathetic?
2. Is church a place you go on Sunday morning (or don't go at all) and forget about the rest of the week?
3. Does church represent a set of rules, or a relationship?
4. Do you think the only effective time to go to church is on Sunday morning? Why or why not?

WHAT OTHERS MAY THINK

Sunday is:

a. The day when football is on ALL day and no other plans better be made. Peanuts, pretzels, and beer are mandatory.

  b. The one day of the week everyone heaves a huge sigh of
     relief because they can sleep in.
  c. The day that if your grandmother is in town you will defi-
     nitely, definitely have to go to church wearing your
     Sunday best.
  d. The day you gather with other believers to worship God.

There is something special about being at church on Sunday
morning. There are other people with you as part of a community. You
are not alone. There is something powerful about what we refer to as
"corporate worship" (and no, it has nothing to do with the world of business). It is a group of people who gather to worship God at a set time,
once a week.

I miss it when I am not at church, worshipping on a Sunday morning.
If I am out of town and can't worship with my home church on a Sunday
I can "make it up" by listening to a CD or download of the service, but
something definitely gets lost. The recording only picks up the singers
with microphones during the music praise portion of the service; the
tape is not able to record the expressions on people's faces touched by a
part of the message; and it certainly doesn't convey the personal interactions: hugs, encouragements, or smiles.

How important do you think it is to worship at a local church? Why?

A NEW WAY TO BELIEVE

Look at Psalm 118:22. What (or who) is the capstone referred to in
this verse? (This same passage is quoted in the New Testament in 1 Peter
2:7.)

Now read Psalm 122:1. What do you think "house of the Lord"
refers to?

Read Ephesians 5:23. Who is head of the church?

What connection do you see between the capstone, the church and the church as the body of believers?

Josh Harris writes in his book *Stop Dating the Church*:

> Every Christian is called to be passionately committed to a specific local church. Why? Because the local church is the key to spiritual health and growth for a Christian. And because as the visible "body of Christ: in the world, the local church is central to God's plan for every generation . . . a wholehearted relationship with a local church is God's loving plan for me and for every other follower of Christ."

Do you agree or disagree?

In what ways can the local church be a key to spiritual health and growth?

What encompasses a "wholehearted relationship" with the local church?

Have you experienced this kind of relationship with a local church?

What does Galatians 6:2 say?

Which of the following apply to you and the relationship you have now with a specific church?

   __ I don't have one and I don't need one.
   __ I don't have one because I am too busy, but I watch church on TV.
   __ I go to church on Sundays, but only because I feel guilty if I don't.

___ I go to church on Sundays and usually get something out of it, especially when it is fellowship Sunday. Then I get a good meal!

___ I have a total commitment to God, and can't wait to go to church on Sunday morning to worship him.

If you have one, are you satisfied with your relationship with a local church? Why or why not?

BELIEVE AND ACT

· If you don't already have one, consider finding a local church where you can worship, serve, and fellowship with others.

· How? Ask a friend you know who goes to church if you can go with him some Sunday.

· Remember, the church located on the street corner closest to your home may not be the best choice (location should not be the determining factor).

ASK THROUGH PRAYER

Thank you, Jesus, for being the capstone of the church and creating local churches, as well as the universal church, which is the body of believers. Help me find a local church where I can meet you face-to-face and receive the love, mercy, and grace you so freely give.

Amen.

Day Four:

The Bible Really Is the Good Book!

THOUGHT FOR THE DAY

The Bible is more than just a blueprint for life, a set of moral tales, and a collection of prose and poetry. It also contains steamy tales of betrayal and lust, revenge and murder, and intrigue and adventure that keep you turning the pages.

WHAT DO YOU BELIEVE?

1. Has there ever been a time in your life when you have read the Bible on a regular basis? If so, when? And what motivated you?
2. Do you think the Bible is a useful guide for "right living?"
3. Do you think the Bible is as relevant today as it was 2,000 years ago? Why or why not?

WHAT OTHERS MAY THINK

The Bible is:

a. A book I probably should read but was more applicable to my grandmother than to me.
b. A book full of thee's and thou's and all kinds of other words and sayings I don't understand.

    c. The book you can find inside the top drawer of any hotel room.

    d. God's inspired living and Holy Word that serves as our blueprint for life.

I received my first Bible when I was nineteen or twenty as a gift from my future husband's parents. I awkwardly accepted what I knew was a meaningful gift but really didn't know what to think of it or what to do with it.

They hoped I would read it but didn't give me any guidance about where to start. My Bible knowledge was limited to knowing there was an Old Testament and a New Testament, but that was about it. I didn't know that the original language of the Old Testament was Hebrew or that the New Testament had originally been written in Greek. As a matter of fact, the whole book was Greek to me, and it was fine with me if it stayed that way.

It didn't help that the version they presented me with was the King James Version. Maybe if it had been written in an easier-to-understand style I would have been more interested but I'm not sure.

You see, I had some pretty solid preconceived notions about what the Bible was and was not.

Do you have preconceived impressions about what the Bible is? Describe them.

Do you believe that the Bible is God's inspired Word, and as such is completely true? Why or why not?

What does 2 Samuel 22:31 say about God's Word?

Can truth and flawlessness co-exist?

Do you think it matters which translation of the Bible you read? Why or why not?

My preconceived notions (and this was me, I speak only for myself here) were that the Bible was a pretty dusty, stodgy piece of work that contained lots of thee's and thou's and was written in archaic English that was difficult to wade through.

When I opened the King James Version I was not disappointed. It *was* full of thee's and thou's and was hard to understand. Word economy was absent and when I got to the lineage chapters full of *begots* and *begats* I closed the pages for good.

As a teenager in the late 1970s I needed something more current and to the point. Where were the contemporary translations when I needed them?

Look up the following Bible verses in the King James Version, New International Version, and *The Message*, and compare them. (I've found www.Biblegateway.com a big help for things like this.)

Psalm 37:4
Jeremiah 29:11
John 15:24
Romans 8:28

Do all three versions say the same thing to you? Is one easier for you to understand? Would any sway you toward reading the Bible more (or away from it)?

Is the Bible a book to read:

__ Only when looking for a specific answer to a question?
__ At Christmas and Easter?
__ When you are planning on going to church?

___ When you have time?
___ Weekly?
___ Daily?

A NEW WAY TO BELIEVE

Look up the following verses. What does each verse tell you about God's Word?

Psalm 119:9

Psalm 119:11

Psalm 119:105

Proverbs 30:5

2 Corinthians 4:2

Hebrews 4:12

James 1:22

Deuteronomy 11:18

Matthew 24:35

Which of those verses about God's Word, the Bible, excites you the most? Why?

BELIEVE AND ACT

How do you think it would change your life to "fix these words of mine (God)" in your heart?

What does Matthew 6:21 say about your heart?

I have to admit that when I started to think about "fixing God's words" in my heart, my attitude started to change. Think about the implications a change of heart can have on your relationships:

- The next time you know you are right instead of getting into an argument, let it go.
- Are you predictable in your reactions to certain situations? The next time one of those situations comes up, surprise everyone with a different response.
- Pick a friend you can partner with to read your Bible more consistently than you do now.

ASK THROUGH PRAYER
God,

Thank you for your Word. Thank you for caring about me so much that you communicate your word to me through the Bible. Instill in me a hunger and thirst for the Scriptures, and the desire to store your words in my heart and put them into action in my life.

Amen.

Day Five:

Tearing Down Walls with Your Hands and Feet

THOUGHT FOR THE DAY

Feeling as if we don't belong at church is a barrier that can prevent us from developing a relationship with a faith community (and with Christ).

WHAT DO YOU BELIEVE?

1. Has there ever been a situation when you have been at church and felt totally clueless?
2. Has there ever been a time at church when you didn't understand certain words or terms being used?
3. Did those experiences influence whether you returned?
4. Would it have made a difference if there had been someone with you to "coach" you through?
5. Has there been a time you have gone to a new church and no one acknowledged or greeted you?

WHAT OTHERS MAY THINK

Rituals are:
a. The way things have ALWAYS been done and ain't nothing gonna change that.

b. What my teenage daughter goes through every morning when she gets ready for school. Several items of clothing, hair product, and types of body spray and/or lotion are part of the process.
c. All the up-and-down, up-and-down that happens in church on a Sunday morning that totally confuses me and bothers my knees.
d. Barriers that may exist for people when they attend church.

I remember most of my childhood experiences with church as boring and stifling. It was no place to be a kid. The problem was I still felt that way when I returned sporadically through my early adult years. The service and atmosphere were stifling, boring, reserved, ritualistic, and impossible to understand. The people at church seemed to speak a foreign language: *Christianese*. It was bad enough sitting through tedium and listening to a bunch of people sing out of tune, but not understanding chunks of what was being said just added insult to injury.

Fortunately, after more than twenty years I returned to church. My family was struggling and I knew there was something missing from my life; I just wasn't sure what it was. I discovered what was missing was a personal relationship with Christ, and the barriers to Christianity began to be demolished for me that day. Unfortunately, sometimes barriers take a long, long time to be torn down.

Unfortunately, one barrier I continued to experience, and it stymied my spiritual growth, was Christianese. What were those people in church saying? Thank goodness I'm type A and stuck with it, that's all I have to say.

Christianese is:
a. A foreign language spoken only in church. Might as well be in Babel.
b. Words and phrases that can sound exceptionally judgmental to those who don't understand them.
c. A totally different definition of words we thought we knew.
d. Churchy language that serves to alienate and confuse people who are unfamiliar with church.

Has Christianese ever been a barrier to you in your faith?

When I first went back to church I didn't know the difference between an apostle and an epistle, and had no clue who the "saints" were that people kept referring to.

And the words, "If you have your Bible with you, would you please turn to . . ." were enough to cause me to break out in a cold sweat.

(I will always appreciate (and still use) the following phrase to locate the books of Galatians, Ephesians, Philippians, and Colossians: "Go Eat Pop Corn." A very spiritual statement but hey, if a mnemonic is good enough to use in science class (planets, animal kingdoms, etc.), then why not for Bible study!)

I believe God wants us to communicate clearly with each other. Is there a time you can remember when either Christianese or harsh, judgmental language was used and turned you off to faith?

A NEW WAY TO BELIEVE

If Christians hope to show their faith as attractive, then any barriers to sharing it need to be eliminated. I believe many of those barriers exist in our attitudes and are communicated through our language.

Look up Galatians 5:22-23. What does it say?

How can you communicate each of the following qualities?

· Love

· Joy

· Peace

· Patience

· Kindness

· Goodness

· Faithfulness

· Gentleness

· Self-Control

Which of the following attitudes do you perceive to be barriers to going to church or being attracted to Christianity?

__ Pride	__ Jealousy	__ Criticism
__ Arrogance	__ Anger	__ Ambition
__ Righteousness	__ Humility	__ Patience
__ Intolerance	__ Envy	__ Personal Agenda
__ Truth	__ Hatred	__ Hypercritical Attitude

Have you experienced any of those attitudes, either in a church or from someone who claims to be a Christian? If so, how did it make you feel?

Is this surprising? Why or why not?

What does Ephesians 4:23 say about our attitude if we follow Christ?

List three ways you can be made new in the attitude of your mind:

1.

2.

3.

BELIEVE AND ACT

· Make an effort to relate to those around you in a way they can understand. When talking to kids, speak to them at their level. When communicating faith, remember that actions speak louder than words (and if you are using words, make sure they are easy to understand).

· Nonverbal communication is responsible for communicating more than 70 percent of your message. Is your nonverbal communication in harmony with what you say? Do your tone of voice and body language match your spoken words?

· Pick one quality of the *"fruit of the spirit"* (characteristics listed from Galatians 5:22-23 above) and make a point to focus on it during the coming week.

ASK THROUGH PRAYER

Dear Lord,

Help me to hear, listen to, and understand you, and to communicate your desires and purposes clearly in a spirit of love to those around me.

Amen.

week two:

Answer the Phone
—It's God Calling

God—calling me? No thanks, I don't think I'll answer that phone. If I talk to God, it may take up too much time. Or I may be asked to do something I don't want to. Or the conversation may get a little bit too personal or uncomfortable.

I have to admit, it would be nice to have caller ID that could somehow let me know if God was calling. Why can't it say "God," or display heaven's number? At least I could put myself into a spiritual frame of mind while I decide if I will answer the call. Or plan the conversation—a one-way conversation. It would be fine if I could do all the talking, but I'm not so sure about listening, or answering, either, for that matter.

So I put the conversation off . . . maybe indefinitely or maybe until it just fits into my schedule a little bit better. Perhaps I can put it off 'til next week, when I vow to go to church to get my weekly dose of guilt absolution.

But God wants to call me, have me answer, and engage me in conversation. And that is called prayer. And it should be a first choice, not a last resort.

But prayer had always meant something else to me.

My friend Abby used to close every conversation with me by saying, "I'll be praying for you."

It might be a bit strong to say I hated it, but I really didn't like it. It made me feel uneasy and second-rate, like I really was a black sheep. (Before I came to faith, unbeknown to me, there were several people praying for me.)

"Stop it already with this 'I'll pray for you' stuff (okay, I used a stronger word). It gives me the heebie-jeebies," I said, awkwardly shifting my weight from one foot to the other, refusing to lock eyes with her. You see, if I looked at her, she might actually see my desperate need for prayer, which I so flippantly dismissed.

God wasn't ready to let me off the hook. If I didn't respond to one call, perhaps he could get through with another.

God pursues us through our busy-ness and denial; he longs to engage us in conversation followed by obedience and service, and he longs for us to join a community of others who engage in conversation and service with him. He loves it when we roll up our sleeves and go about his business rather than simply observing from the sideline.

Finally I picked up the phone, answered the call, and started the conversation.

So the next time you think you hear God calling, why not answer and see what he wants to talk with you about?

Why Can't I Just Leave a Message?

THOUGHT FOR THE DAY

Have you thought about a relationship with God that requires active participation on your part, or just one where you talk to him? If I can just leave a message with God, why can't he just do the same with me? Why does he want an answer from me?

WHAT DO YOU BELIEVE?

1. How can you communicate with God?
2. Does God really want you to talk to him?
3. What about obedience—what does that mean?

WHAT OTHERS MAY THINK

Prayer is:

a. What you did a lot of as a teenager hoping your parents wouldn't find out where you really were or what you were really doing.

b. What you add to a wing when you are really desperate and have no idea how to get out of a sticky situation.

c. Your laundry list of requests to God that you expect him to fulfill as if he were Santa or a genie in a bottle.

d. Conversation with God that involves the true heartfelt communication of speaking and listening to him.

What is your prayer life like? X marks the spot:

__ Never
__ Rarely
__ When desperate
__ Sometimes
__ Two or three times a week
__ Daily
__ More than once a day

Were you brought up to include time with God in your day? If so, how much, and how did you feel about it? Did you enjoy spending time with God, or was it something you were forced to do?

Would you like to pray more often? Why or why not?

What motivates you to pray? (Check all that apply.)

__ Guilt
__ Need
__ Desire
__ Being asked
__ Desperation
__ A sense of obligation
__ Sincerely wanting to

I was pretty good at dismissing prayer. I didn't really know what it was, or what it was for, except that it seemed like a more direct link to (hopefully) getting one's own way.

Prayers I had heard seemed pretty shallow. They were rote requests void of feeling and full of expectation. They usually followed a formula complete with a few pious words thrown in for good measure. The prayers amounted to a litany of requests with a couple of gratuitous but shallow thank-yous thrown in to prompt a positive response just a bit sooner than prayers that didn't include "please" and "thank you."

Wrong. But it took some learning to get it right.

Read Matthew 6:5-8. What does that passage have to say about prayer?

List ways you should pray:

List ways you should not pray:

Based on the Scripture above:

Where can you pray?

To whom should you pray?

Write a sample prayer:

Does God know what we need before we ask?

Do you find this hard to believe? Why or why not?

A NEW WAY TO BELIEVE

Look up the following Scripture verses and tell how they help you believe that God knows what you need before you even ask for it.

Jeremiah 1:5

Psalm 139:4

Psalm 139:15

Proverbs 5:21

Romans 8:27

Can one-word prayers be effective? Why or why not?

Have you ever used one-word prayers (and realized that was what you were doing)? Have you ever cried out, "Please!" or "Help!"?

What if you don't know how to pray? Can you still pray even if you don't have the words? Jot your thoughts down here and then read Romans 8:26. What does this verse say?

In the Lord's Prayer, Jesus teaches us how to pray. When I was young and went to church with my great-grandmother, I would recite this prayer, but it was just empty words. It also seemed like a favorite prayer to recite at weddings and funerals, but the words remained hollow.

Yet there is so much wisdom and instruction from Jesus in this prayer.

The Lord's Prayer is found in Matthew 6:9-13, and Jesus opens with instructions: "This, then, is how you should pray." The Lord's Prayer is written below. In the space provided, write the important features of the prayer and how you can include them when you pray.

"Our Father in heaven,

Hallowed be your name,

Your kingdom come,

Your will be done

On earth as it is in heaven.

Give us today our daily bread.

Forgive us our debts,

As we also have forgiven our debtors.

And lead us not into temptation,

But deliver us from the evil one.

What about listening? Is this as important as asking in prayer? Why or why not?

What do the following verses have to say about listening?

· Deuteronomy 30:20

· 1 Samuel 3:9

· Proverbs 12:15

BELIEVE AND ACT

- · God may be calling you to his purpose, but if you don't listen you may not hear his voice.
- · List three quiet places where you can pray. Remember-you can pray anytime, anywhere.
- · Prayer is a conversation.

ASK THROUGH PRAYER

Holy God,

Thank you for wanting to have a conversation with me. I want to communicate with you. Please teach me how to do this.

Amen.

DAY TWO:

Is Your Line Always Busy, or Can God Get Through?

THOUGHT FOR THE DAY

If God wants to speak with you, will you hear and recognize his voice, or are you too busy?

WHAT DO YOU BELIEVE?

1. Do you think God wants to speak with you?
2. Do you think you can only hear God's voice during a prescribed quiet time?
3. Do you think quiet time with God has to take place at a certain time in a certain way?
4. Are the other things you are busy doing as important as spending time with God?
5. Did your parents spend time with God?

WHAT OTHERS MAY THINK

Call is:

a. When you were a teeny-bopper waiting for from the really cute guy.

b. What you dread in the middle of the night when you have teenagers.
c. Something there will be entirely too much of in your future if you have "tween" daughters.
d. God's communication and direction for your life.

When I first told people God talked to me, I got some pretty interesting reactions (like I must have had three heads and none of them had ears). It quickly became obvious I needed to qualify that statement and assure people I don't hear audible voices. It is more like a nudge, or a strong feeling that won't go away, to do something NOW! Yes, I absolutely believe that God talks to me.

When God talked to me about sharing our son's issues with substance abuse in a book, I quickly did what I refer to as the "Moses dance"—a "you gotta be kidding, not me, no how, no way" reaction. Later this week we'll talk about obedience, so more on that then. In the meantime, I would like you to think about how God speaks to you.

What are some of the ways God has "spoken" to you?

If you haven't heard God's voice, what do you think are some of the reasons why you haven't?

When I was baptized, I shared Jeremiah 29:11 as a verse that is significant to me: "'For I know the plans I have for you,' declares the LORD, 'plans to prosper you and not to harm you, plans to give you hope and a future.'" I loved the fact that God had a plan for me, a plan that included hope for the future, prosperity, and protection.

I also recognized plenty of times in my life when I got in the way of God's plans for me, by getting so busy I squeezed him right out and took control. This was especially easy to do when things were going well.

The biggest barrier I put up was simply not including God in my day. I was very comfortable in the saddle of self-sufficiency. Leave it to me! I could handle it, whatever "it" was. God didn't give me a husband whose name was Pride for nothing!

What do the following Scripture verses have to say about spending time with God? What happens when we spend time with God?

Proverbs 2:6

Colossians 1:10

James 1:5

How do you feel about spending time with God?

How important do you think it is to spend time with God when things are going well?

What about when things are not going so well?

Do you think you need to spend time with God at a particular time of day? If so, when? For how long?

What are some of the barriers that prevent you from spending regular time with God?

A NEW WAY TO BELIEVE
What do the following Scripture verses say about God's availability to us?

· Joshua 1:5

· Hebrews 13:5

Do you believe God is available 24/7?

What does Zephaniah 3:17 say about God's desire to spend time with us?

What are some ways you can spend time with God so you can hear his voice?

I noticed that once I got my own agenda out of the way, I was able to be quiet so I could hear God's voice. One of the best ways to become quiet before God is to get your focus off yourself and onto him.

What are some of the ways you can focus on God instead of yourself?

Is there a time of day you would most likely be able to dedicate some time alone with God? If so, when?

List five habits you can develop to hear God's voice:

1.
2.
3.
4.
5.

List five barriers to hearing God's voice:

1.

2.

3.

4.

5.

BELIEVE AND ACT
· There are several ways to hear God's voice.
· Reflect on settings in which you feel most able to hear God's voice.
· Busy-ness can be a way to avoid pain in your life; seek God's answers instead.
· Believe that God wants to communicate with you.

ASK THROUGH PRAYER
Thank you, God, for wanting to have a relationship with me. Thank you for calling me to a life with you and having a purpose for me. Help me give up my agenda and follow your plan so you can work in my life. Thank you that I can find you always.
Amen.

Day Three:

Cancel the Call-Waiting and Sign Up for Speed Dial

THOUGHT FOR THE DAY

Prayer is a powerful conduit through which God releases his blessing, and should be accessed as a first choice, not a last resort.

WHAT DO YOU BELIEVE?

1. Do you go to prayer first, or as a last resort?
2. Does God always answer prayer?
3. How does God answer prayer?
4. Can bad things or difficult situations be answers to prayer?

WHAT OTHERS MAY THINK

Petition is:

a. A piece of paper my mother collected signatures on in the 1960s to get people to stop clubbing baby seals.
b. A way to interact with the courts when you seek to get your own way.
c. A fancy name for argument.
d. Presenting our requests humbly before God.

"I'm praying for you; I will pray for you; you're in my prayers . . ."

Okay, I admit that when life gets messy, I usually remember to pray for others. But when things calm down, or when God answers, I am prone to getting a little bit sloppy or lazy in my requests (and praises, for that matter).

I don't know how many times I have heard someone say, "There's nothing else to do but pray." My observation and experience is that making that comment usually means we've tried everything else under the sun to fix the problem ourselves and we're throwing our hands up in despair and resorting to what should have been the first choice. But then again, I'm a total control freak and would love to get credit for solving the world's problems.

So at some point we remember to pray. We get those requests (more like demands) out on the table and wait for God to magically appear like a summoned genie and take care of things, the sooner the better. As a matter of fact, yesterday wouldn't be a minute too soon.

But wait a minute.

I expect God to answer me pronto—but did I go to him pronto? Or did I resort to prayer as some pathetic, last-ditch option? How many times have we heard people say with a huge sigh, not really believing it will make any difference, "Well, all I can do is pray."

I readily admit I'm still waiting for some answers, and I don't always like the answers God gives me. I suppose that's why I like to take matters into my own hands and try to solve problems myself. But when I do I usually just end up prolonging the wait.

When you have a need, how soon do you pray?

__ Right away
__ When I get around to it
__ When someone suggests it
__ As a last resort

When you pray, do you believe God will answer? Why or why not?

If your belief meter is running low, you can also pray about that. Look up Mark 9:24. Is there a time you've prayed this prayer?

Which of the following time frames do you believe God uses to answer prayer?

___ Immediate
___ Not yet
___ Not at all

When God chooses the "not yet" option I take encouragement from the story of Abraham and Sarah, who waited a LONG, LONG time for their prayer for a child to be answered. You can read their story in Genesis 21:1-7. I would rather have immediate answers, but then again, I'll take "not yet" over "not at all."

Psalm 27:13-14 is also an encouragement: *"I am still confident of this: I will see the goodness of the LORD in the land of the living. Wait for the LORD; be strong and take heart and wait for the LORD."*

What does Matthew 6:33 say to you?

How can you seek the kingdom of God?

Do you think prayer is one way of seeking the kingdom of God?

Do you forget to pray? Do you pray as a last resort? If so, check all that may apply to you:

___ Unbelief
___ Self-sufficiency
___ Pride
___ Forgetfulness

___ Fatigue
___ Lack of knowledge how to pray
___ Laziness

Look up the following Scripture passages and match them with the reasons (or excuses) above:

Ephesians 5:15-16

Mark 9:24

Proverbs 16:18

Romans 8:26

James 5:11

Psalm 103:2

Proverbs 19:21

A NEW WAY TO BELIEVE

One day it finally dawned on me that maybe God really *did* know better than me about what was best. But I only remember this when I keep my meddling fingers out of the mix (and someone as type A and control-freakish as I am needs a lot of reminders).

Read Romans 8:28. Put it into your own words:

That verse can serve as a powerful reminder when you are tempted to take matters into your own hands and dismiss God and how he works things out in his timing.

Do you love God? Do you believe he has a purpose for your life? Have you seen bad things work for good in the big picture when you kept your hands off?

God can (and will) use what we in the world perceive as "bad" things as answers to prayer.

I remember when God answered one of my "desperate mom pleas" through my son getting arrested. Yes, you read that right. An arrest was an answer to prayer.

Did you catch that word "desperate?" God knows what's in our heart, and sometimes that's a scary thought. No hiding from him. But rather than zap us for that, he yearns to reach out to us with compassion and blessings—if our hearts and motivation are pure.

Look up 1 Samuel 16:7. If God looked at your heart right now, what would he find?

If you need a heart transplant you can pray Psalm 51:10 to God. What does this verse say?

What do you need to let go of to have a pure heart?

To have a steadfast spirit?

You can also pray Psalm 86:11.

What might you need to let go of to have an undivided heart?

BELIEVE AND ACT
· I have heard it takes twenty-eight days to develop a habit. For the next month, first thing each morning ask God to join you. Ask him now to remind you if you forget.
· "Letting go and letting God" is a constant process. It's not just a once-and-done action.
· Ask others to pray that you would seek God first and not last.

UnDoing Church

· When you offer to pray for others, keep your commitment
 and pray, meaning it and believing it.

ASK THROUGH PRAYER
God,

Thank you for knowing what is best for me even when I don't believe that you do. Thank you for being willing to help me through my unbelief. And thank you for answering my prayers even if it's not according to my schedule. Help me truly believe in you and put you on speed dial, rather than on hold.

Amen.

DAY FOUR:

Do I Have to Be on the Phone Chain?

THOUGHT FOR THE DAY
God is a master communicator and uses several styles to reach us, hoping we will be obedient.

WHAT DO YOU BELIEVE?
1. When you sense God prompting you to do something, do you follow through or do you put it off?
2. What does obedience really mean?
3. Does being obedient to God scare you?
4. Do you really believe God expects you to obey him when he speaks to you?
5. Do you believe there are blessings (rewards) in store for you when you obey?

WHAT OTHERS MAY THINK
Obedience is:
a. What they call training school for your canine friends.
b. What your Catholic school teacher (especially if she was a nun in her late seventies) expected from you when you were in kindergarten.

    c. What hard-nosed higher-ups demand from subordinates.

    d. What God requires of you to fulfill the purpose of your life, which includes his desire to grant you an abundant life with many blessings.

I don't like the word obedience. It's stronger than "following" or "taking a suggestion." The implication in my mind is that it requires giving up something I like or find comfortable or believe in. I think it might be first cousins with sacrifice.

What's especially tough about being obedient to God is that he has a unique way of looking at things. God looks at things differently than pop culture does. And we live in a world where we are surrounded by pop culture and its messages. If you don't believe me, in John 18:36 Jesus says, *"My kingdom is not of this world."*

But most of us don't get it right the first time. And you will be happy to know that some of God's heroes didn't get it right the first time either. Take Moses, for example.

Here's Moses, an *"alien in a foreign land"* (Exodus 2:22), a Hebrew brought up in Egypt by the pharaoh's daughter. He takes matters into his own hands and ends up fleeing Egypt for his life (Exodus 2:12-15).

And then God calls and Moses tries not to answer the phone.

What does God say to Moses in Exodus 3:10?

How does Moses answer in verse 11?

Have you ever argued with God and tried to avoid his plans? Have you ever danced the Moses dance? If so, when?

Has God ever asked you to do something and you felt unqualified? Does it matter what God is asking of you? How did Moses answer God in Exodus 4:10? Did Moses feel qualified?

But God loves the weak and "unqualified." (I heaved a huge sigh of relief with this discovery!)

What does God tell you in 1 Corinthians 12:22 about the "weaker parts of the body"?

In 2 Corinthians 12:10, what does Paul say he delights in?

A NEW WAY TO BELIEVE

Ah, but there was a turning point for Moses, and that was when he stopped arguing and decided to obey.

The Bible tells another great story of obedience and what happens when we don't obey God's call.

Meet Jonah, handpicked by God to perform a job, a job that involved going to Nineveh—a city about which God said, "Its wickedness has come up before me" (Jonah 1:2).

How did Jonah respond? God gives us the answer not once, but twice in verse 3. God tells us Jonah "ran away" from him, and then tells us Jonah "fled" from him aboard a ship.

Have you ever run away from God? In what circumstances?

How did God respond in verse 4?

What kind of consequences to disobedience have you experienced?

What did Jonah finally decide in verse 12?

Did the crew of the ship follow Jonah's advice? What happened then?

Have there been times when you have been ready to acknowledge your bad choices, but others got in the way of letting you experience the consequences (often referred to as "enabling")?

What did Jonah do after he finally suffered the consequences of his actions and ended up as fish food (2:1)?

What did God do in verse 10?

Have there been situations like this in your life when you finally obeyed, prayed, and experienced God's answer?

The next time God asked Jonah to do something, how did he respond (3:3)?

Did you respond the same way Jonah did the next time God asked you to do something, or did you argue some more?

Not only did Jonah obey, but the Ninevites believed and obeyed as well. What was God's reaction (verse 10)?
Are there times you have been obedient and experienced God's compassion?

Oh-h-h-h, but it's so hard to be obedient, especially when you can't see the end result, or you have trouble letting go of your own agenda, or it seems as if God is asking you to do something you think is risky or unreasonable. Where does Romans 1:5 say obedience comes from?

Refresh your memory. The definition of faith can be found in Hebrews 11:1-2. What is it?

And faith brings righteousness, or being made right with God. What does Romans 3:22 say?

How important is obedience to God? Look up 1 Samuel 15:22. What does it say?

As you ponder today's lesson, does a connection between obedience, faith, and blessing emerge for you? Take a moment to jot down your thoughts:

Do you agree with the following?

__ Disobedience yields consequence.
__ Obedience yields blessing.
__ Faith develops obedience.
__ Obedience honors God.

BELIEVE AND ACT
· Remember that in God's eyes obedience is better than sacrifice.
· As you become better at hearing God's voice, try to argue less and obey more.
· Remember that obedience is developed through faith.
· As you become better at hearing and recognizing God's voice, it will become less difficult to obey.

ASK THROUGH PRAYER
God,
Help me! Because I am an imperfect person I tend to like to have my own way and believe that I am correct. Help me become more adept at hearing your voice and most importantly be obedient to your call.
Amen.

DAY Five:

Let's Make It a Conference Call

THOUGHT FOR THE DAY
You can worship anytime and anyplace, but worshipping with others is important, too.

WHAT DO YOU BELIEVE?
1. What are the advantages of worshipping in community?
2. What is corporate worship?
3. How can going to a Bible study enhance worship?

WHAT OTHERS MAY THINK
Sunday Morning Service is:
a. Where people can go to empty their guilt buckets and wipe away their sins of the week.
b. Where weary parents can go to veg out on Sunday morning and send their kid to the nursery (but only if the service starts after 10 a.m.).
c. A place where church insiders learn how to insulate themselves more from the outside world.

    d. A welcoming community of learners, open to all to explore God's Word and how it is alive and relevant in today's world.

I hated going to church as a kid. It was a place I rarely attended, it was full of rules, and I had to wear Mary Jane shoes that were inevitably too tight and left me with blisters, and my lace trimmed socks always itched.

I was bored, wasn't allowed to color, and found nothing inspiring about listening to a group of tone-deaf individuals singing, followed by an older guy droning on and on.

When I tried church again as a young adult, it wasn't much better. It highlighted my spiritual ignorance. When the pastor referred to a particular book of the Bible, I either snuck a look at the index, or tried to peek over my neighbor's shoulder. I felt like I was a school kid cheating on a test. I had no clue where the book of Colossians or Ruth could be found, and generally felt like a second-class citizen. It was as if Sunday church service was some special kind of club with its own rules and language.

But worship within a local church is important. To develop fellowship and community is one of God's top priorities for us.

Did you go to church growing up? How would you describe the services?

Do you attend church now? If so, is it different from when you were younger?

If you had not attended church in the past, or you had been away from church for a while and went back, what prompted you to go?

What do you see as the benefits of going to church?

Do you think Jesus wants us to worship as part of a group?

How do you define *community*?

How important is it to you to go to church on Sunday morning (or whenever the service is held)?
__ Not at all
__ A little
__ Somewhat
__ Very
__ Critical

How important is it to God that you attend church (worship in community)?

A NEW WAY TO BELIEVE
During the first week, we discussed the concept that church isn't a building, rather a group of committed followers of Christ. What is important is that we meet, not where we meet.

Where are some places you may meet for church?

Before discussing the concept of corporate (community) worship further, it is important to recognize several reasons why individuals may not be able to break away and attend community worship at a prescribed time or place. List them here:

Do you think a certain number of people need to be present to worship God in community? What does Jesus say in Matthew 18:20 about being present with worshippers?

What do you believe the church's mission is? Check all that apply:

___ To protect Christians from the sinful influences of the world

___ To be a meeting/gathering place for praise and worship

___ To be a conduit of God's love to each other and hurting people outside

___ To be an alternative social setting

___ To be a place to simply escape from it all once a week

___ To be a place where you can go to wipe any guilt away

___ To be a place that exists to make you feel better, no strings attached

If you go to church, why do you attend?

BELIEVE AND ACT
· Spend some time thinking about the characteristics of authentic community that are important to you, and explore to discover if there are local churches that demonstrate those characteristics.
· How can you contribute to building a worship community?
· Are there two or three others who can help you prayerfully find a local church?

ASK THROUGH PRAYER
Father God,

You are the essence of community. Help me find a local community where I can grow in my relationship with you and be a living, breathing part of your family. Help me serve you through the community of a local church.

Amen.

week three:

Traveling God's Roadways

I used to think the Christian life was dull, chock full of rules, with a bunch of straight-laced biddies who also happened to enjoy and be very good at gossiping. And that wasn't for me.

What I have found is that the Christian life is more like a roller coaster, complete with precipitous drops, inversions, and backward loops before delivering you safely to the exit platform. It is a great adventure into uncharted territory that one minute may have you screaming at the top of your lungs from surprise, or even fear, and the next minute whooping in joyful exuberance.

The journey is full of U-turns, dead ends, one-way streets, potholes, detours, red lights, and sometimes no map. But it is a grand adventure full of surprises and unimaginable vistas!

I never would have believed it until I lived it. God has taken me to the most amazing and desperate places. Okay, I don't like the word desperate either, but not all the travel will be first-class; some of it might be standby, delayed, or maybe even cancelled. There may be times the journey leaves you stuck in one place, much like being stranded at an airport with no flight out, for hours or even days. (And they sent your luggage on ahead, or even worse, lost it!)

My journey with God started when I came to the end of myself. Thrown off the horse of self-sufficiency, I landed squarely on my derriere in desperation. My son was smoking weed and had become belligerent. I was hopeless and lost, no map or plan in sight. Yet God had the map and took me on the journey. He had everything under control.

The problem is, we try to figure things out on our own. Which way are we going? I want to be in the driver's seat. Let Jesus be the pilot? Uh, no thanks, I want that control. And you mean I might have to slow down and travel according to someone else's schedule? No! And, worse yet, detour while God teaches me yet another lesson? And did I mention I'm a slow learner?

Is there a journey God wants to lead you through? Are you willing to be a passenger? (If you are anything like me, the answer is no.) But maybe you're willing to take a chance on the adventure of a lifetime? I hope so. Let's go for a ride!

We'll visit five landmark destinations of the Christian life. So come along and take in the sights!

Day one:

Was This Road on the Map, or Am I Lost?

THOUGHT FOR THE DAY

There are times when we are totally lost, yet we are exactly where God wants or needs us to be. This flew in the face of what I had always believed: that living as a Christian guaranteed a life on Easy Street. After all, I had access to God, who had created everything and could certainly ensure my needs (wants) were met. Boy, did I have a thing or two to learn! God, like a loving parent, set boundaries for me.

WHAT DO YOU BELIEVE?

- Have you ever felt as if you were in an impossible situation and that you couldn't possibly see a way out or see a silver lining, but in retrospect you recognized God's hand?
- Do you believe that God knows your entire life story from beginning to end?
- What does the term desert experience mean to you?

WHAT OTHERS MAY THINK

Desert is:
a. Dessert misspelled.

b. Someplace way off where I will never, ever go.
c. What more and more of the earth will turn into if global warming doesn't stop.
d. Valley experiences God allows so we will open our hearts to him.

Not only am I not always a quick learner—sometimes I never seem to learn, and make the same mistake over and over. When our younger son was a teenager, he smoked a lot of pot. It became so bad he was court-ordered out of our home, yet for months I would enable him and deny the extent of his problem. I was repeating the same mistake over and over again and not learning from the desert experience I had been dealt.

A definition of insanity is repeating the same action while expecting a different result. Yet sometimes I spend months or even years (for some people it is a lifetime), not learning the intended lesson—to take a different approach—which might yield a different outcome.

The Bible contains stories of desert experiences, including that of the Israelites wandering in the heat of the desert for forty years. Forty years! They kept repeating the same mistakes and didn't get it! God gave them repeated opportunities to make good choices but they still blew it and finally God had had enough.

Read Numbers 32:13. Why did God make the Israelites wander in the desert for forty years?

How did they show contempt for God in each of the following verses?

· Exodus 16:3
· Exodus 16:20
· Numbers 11:1
· Numbers 11:4
· Numbers 14:1
· Numbers 14:2
· Numbers 14:3

· Numbers 14:4
· Numbers 14:11

What common thread do you see in the Scripture verses above?

Can you remember a time when you made the same mistake over and over again? What was it?

Did you grumble and complain about it or did you learn a valuable lesson? How long did it take? Or are you still learning?

A NEW WAY TO BELIEVE
List some other words for desert:

Why do you think God allows us to enter the desert and sometimes stay there for extended periods?

What do you think he may want you to learn?

How do you think God would prefer we respond?

Read James 1:6-7. How are we told to respond to trials? Why?

What will we develop as a result?

How will perseverance help?

If we are still lacking something, what should we do?

What conditions exist when we seek wisdom?

What happens if faith is absent or when we doubt?

Think back to a time (retrospection is a valuable teacher) when you faced a test or challenge that came at you from all sides. Can you identify the gift you received as a result of that experience?

When our son wouldn't stop smoking marijuana, it brought me to the end of myself. I continued to make many mistakes, but I did receive a wonderful, wonderful gift: the gift of a personal relationship with Jesus. It was through that incredibly difficult desert experience I came to faith in Christ and accepted him not only as my Lord, but as my Savior as well

BELIEVE AND ACT
· It is difficult to see the good that can come out of a miserable situation when you are in the middle of it. Pat answers and platitudes won't go far in supporting your friends.
· If the desert experience is yours, persevere and cling to hope. If you want to encourage someone else, follow the other person's lead and try not to tell her what to do or how to feel.

· The following Scriptures are worth living by:

Exodus 14:14 (and I need this translation, from *The Message*, to get the point through my thick head): "*GOD will fight the battle for you. And you? You keep your mouths shut!*"

2 Corinthians 1:3, 4 (also from The Message): *"All praise to the God and Father of our Master, Jesus the Messiah! Father of all mercy! God of all healing counsel! He comes alongside us when we go through hard times, and before you know it, he brings us alongside someone else who is going through hard times so that we can be there for that person just as God was there for us."*

ASK THROUGH PRAYER

God,

Thanks for always being there, even if I don't recognize you or acknowledge you. Sooner or later you will get my attention and I will be able to love and care for others in the way you have loved and cared for me. I will learn to be thankful for the desert experiences (because that gratitude does not come naturally), and use those hurts and comforts to bring glory to you.

Amen.

DAY TWO:

Speed Limits Strictly Enforced

THOUGHT FOR THE DAY

Keep in mind that no matter how much we disagree, God's timing is always perfect. If we try to get out ahead of him by taking things into our own hands, there can be some nasty consequences, or at least a visit to the closest desert.

WHAT DO YOU BELIEVE?
· Will God slow you down if you get ahead of him?
· Do you agree with the statement, "God's timing is always perfect"?
· Do you think God really knows what's best for you?
· How might God's purpose for your life get derailed?

WHAT OTHERS MAY THINK
Answered prayer is:
a. When my kids let me sleep in on Saturday mornings.
b. What I expect from God, like answered wishes from a genie.
c. When my friend digs me out of an impossible situation.

d. When God's plans and purposes unfold in my life according to his will, in his timing.

I am a bona fide, class A, number one control freak. It suddenly occurred to me one day that I was not in charge of the world. I may have come to this realization, but I often forget to live by it.

The fact is I don't usually like God's timing. He operates according to his own clock, which is usually based on whether I am listening and obedient, and absorbing what he is trying to teach me. It seems I have a hearing problem—and then a doing problem as well—especially when the direction I am being pointed in doesn't seem to make much sense to me. That may be the first clue that God is directing: It usually isn't the way I would handle things.

I have found that God's answers typically fall into one of three categories: "Yes," "No," or "Slow." I don't *usually* have a problem with "Yes" (although I also admit to wanting quick answers or direction according to what I think is best), but I definitely don't like "No" or "Slow."

Have there been times in your life when you have totally taken charge and found yourself in a mess?

How would you describe yourself?

___ I am a total follower.
___ I like to have a little input.
___ I like to be part of decision making.
___ I like to be an equal partner in decision making.
___ I'm willing to take other's opinions into consideration, but want my opinion to prevail.
___ I like to be in total control of a situation.
___ I run the world.

How likely are you to seek counsel from others when making important decisions?

How likely are you to seek counsel from God (through prayer) when making important decisions?

A NEW WAY TO BELIEVE

Think back and list some unique ways God worked out solutions to your problems.

Do you think difficult experiences can be answers to prayer? Why or why not?

Have you ever had an experience where a difficult situation became the solution to a problem you were confronting?

Can your own desires be overridden by others' prayers? Why or why not?

What do the following Scripture verses reveal about prayer and the things that contribute to your prayers being answered?

2 Chronicles 7:14

Romans 8:26

Matthew 6:5

Philippians 4:6

1 Thessalonians 5:17

James 5:16

Does one of these verses jump out at you more than the others, and if so, why?

How might you change the way you pray based on today's material? Do you think you will pray more frequently for others in the future?

How seriously should we take the commitment to pray for others? In other words, if I tell someone, "I will pray for you," how big a deal is it if I don't follow through?

What can you infer by reading Colossians 1:9?

BELIEVE AND ACT
- It is important to follow through on our commitment to pray. Don't promise to pray if you won't be able to keep the promise.
- Persistence in prayer is important. Read the parable of the persistent widow in Luke 18:1-8.
- Don't underestimate the power of prayer.

ASK THROUGH PRAYER
God,

Thank you for your wisdom in answering my prayers. Help me be patient in waiting for your answers. I am not a patient person and would rather have quick if not immediate answers to prayer. Help me understand that I do not know what is best and have only limited understanding and vision, and that you have the big picture and master plan perfectly worked out and that I will only disrupt things if I take matters into my own hands. Continue to help me wait for your perfect answers even and especially when I don't understand.

Amen.

DAY THREE:

WHY ARE THERE SO MANY POTHOLES IN THIS ROAD?

THOUGHT FOR THE DAY

A Christian's life will not be trouble-free. Also, God's people are not perfect. So why do so many churches seem to project perfection: people who appear to have it all together, show up dressed in their proverbial Sunday best, and then cast disdaining looks at those who don't appear to fit in?

When I started reading the Bible, I met David and realized he was far from perfect, yet was a devoted follower of God. (See 1 Samuel 13:14; Acts 13:22.) Why hadn't anyone ever told me about him?

WHAT DO YOU BELIEVE?

· Do you think the Christian life is only made for perfect people?

· Have you attended churches where you were accepted just as you are? Or ones where you felt like you had to put on a "perfect face," or didn't feel accepted for who you are?

· When you're around Christians what are some of the different ways you feel?

WHAT OTHERS MAY THINK
Christian Life is:
a. A boring way of life that is full of things you're not allowed to do.
b. What your friends and relatives tell you you're crazy to want to live.
c. A guarantee of prosperity and life on Easy Street if you pray hard enough.
d. A life dedicated to becoming more and more like Christ as we seek to follow him and serve as his hands and feet on Earth.

Ah-h-h-h . . . the Christian life, Easy Street, full of perfect people leading perfect lives, right? Wrong.

Let me tell you a little of the story of David and Bathsheba. (The entire account can be read in 2 Samuel 11.)

David was a man after God's own heart, yet he had many flaws. He fell in lust with another man's wife, first noticing her beautiful body while she was bathing on her rooftop.

Then he sent someone over to find out about her. He learned her name was Bathsheba, and even though she was another man's wife (a man who was off at battle no less) he had her brought to him. Then they had sex and she got pregnant. And her husband was off at war, so it would be obvious he wasn't the father. I'd say David got himself into a bit of a bind.

No fear. David dreamed up a solution—one that ended up just making a bad situation worse. He summoned Bathsheba's husband, Uriah the Hittite, under the pretense of seeing how the war was going, and would reward him by sending him home to sleep with his wife. No one would be the wiser. David even sent him a gift. Problem solved, so David thought.

Wrong. Bathsheba's husband didn't feel right about sleeping with his wife while all his soldiers were still at battle, so he slept at the palace entrance with all the king's servants. Uh-oh. So David had him stay another night and figured if he got him drunk, surely he would go and sleep with his wife, but he didn't. Now David was really in a jam.

So when Uriah the Hittite went back to battle, David sent a note along with him to give to his commander. What Uriah didn't know was that the note essentially contained his death sentence. What choice did David have but to make sure the poor guy died? In the note he asked his commanding officer to place Uriah in the front line of battle and once he was positioned there have the supporting troops withdraw so he would be killed. No kidding.

But that's not the end of the story. After a period of mourning, Bathsheba was brought to David and they got married.

"But the thing David had done displeased the LORD" (2 Samuel 11:27).

What is the main message communicated to you through this story?

Does it serve as an encouragement, a warning, or both? Why?

Can you relate to any of the bad choices David made?

While most of us have not committed murder, there are several other examples of mistakes David made in this story. For the following questions, refer to 2 Samuel 11.

What other choice than staying in Jerusalem could David have made in verse 1?

Have there been times when you have shirked responsibilities?

What was David guilty of in verses 2 and 3?

Have there been times when you have let your eyes wander and linger over someone?

Did you devise a way to find out more about that person?

Read verses 4 and 5. Have you known people who have gotten into similar binds as David's?

While you may or may not know someone who has gotten someone else's wife pregnant, you might know someone who has committed adultery. Did they try to cover it up and if so for how long and to what lengths did they go?

Have you made mistakes that you have tried to cover up?

In verses 6 through17, what happened when David took matters into his own hands to try to fix the problem? Did it get better, or did things go from bad to worse?

What were some of the mistakes David made?

Can you relate to one small white lie, or one small indiscretion leading to another and before you knew it the situation had gotten way out of control and you were in way over your head?

A NEW WAY TO BELIEVE

I love what the introduction to 1 and 2 Samuel from *The Message* tells us:

> Most of us need to be reminded that these stories are not exemplary in the sense that we stand back and admire them . . . Rather they are immersions into the actual business of living itself: this is what it means to be

human. These four stories [Hannah, Samuel, Saul, and David] do not show us how we should live but how in fact we do live, authenticating the reality of our daily experience as the stuff that God uses to work out his purposes of salvation in us and in the world.

The stories do not do this by talking about God, but . . . [train] us in perceptions of ourselves, our sheer and irreducible humanity that cannot be reduced to personal feelings or ideas or circumstances . . .

One of the many welcome consequences in learning to "read" our lives in the lives of Hannah, Samuel, Saul, and David is a sense of affirmation and freedom: we don't have to fit into prefabricated moral or mental or religious boxes before we are admitted into the company of God—we are taken seriously just as we are given a place in his story, for it is, after all, his story; none of us is the leading character in the story of our life.

Did you learn anything about yourself in David and Bathsheba's story? If so, what?

Did your perception of God change as a result of reading this story?

When thinking about your life experiences and mistakes, have you experienced the sense of affirmation and freedom mentioned above?

Do you perceive the Christian life as one where you don't have to fit into "a prefabricated moral or mental or religious box before [you] are admitted into the company of God"? Why or why not?

Have Christians you have met welcomed you in the same way?

If you are not the leading character in your life, who is?

Can God use our mistakes as part of a Christian life? If so, how? If not, why not?

BELIEVE AND ACT

· Trying to be perfect is not a requirement of the Christian life.
· Acknowledging our mistakes and imperfections, learning from them, and using them to help others are ingredients of a life God will use.
· Transparency in life is much more refreshing than religiosity, especially when wrapped in humility.

ASK THROUGH PRAYER

Dear God,

Help me get rid of acting as if I'm perfect as the definition of the Christian life. Replace it with being open to you and how you will use my life experiences as an encouragement to others, and a testimony to what you can do with all the mistakes I have made and continue to make.

Amen.

DAY FOUR:

DETOUR AHEAD

THOUGHT FOR THE DAY

Even though you go through life with your own plans and agendas, don't be surprised when God takes you in an entirely different direction. Sometimes the detour is just a short one, but sometimes it can be pretty long.

WHAT DO YOU BELIEVE?

· Do you believe God has lessons he would like you to learn in life, or is your life entirely according to your plan?
· Do you believe it's possible that God's detours will be longer if you keep trying to find the shortcuts yourself?
· Do you think God may add more forks in the road to get your attention?

WHAT OTHERS MAY THINK

Lesson is:
a. What my parents, when I was younger and in trouble, said I "would learn, young lady."
b. The forty-five minute period of time set aside weekly for me to learn how to be a master musician.

c. A mis-pronunciation of the word "listen."
d. What God wants me to learn and understand as I become more Christlike.

Before I met the God of mercy, grace, and forgiveness (and yes, accountability, obedience, and discipline, too) I thought my life was my own to do with as I pleased. I was very happy on my high horse of self-sufficiency.

In fact, I tell people I was brought up on the theology of self-sufficiency. My parents love(d) me deeply and wanted the best for me, which included self-reliance, a good education, and a strong desire to achieve. I knew the plans they had for me, and I knew the plans I had for me, but it would be many years before I would know the plans God had for me.

The problem was that even when I first was getting to know Jesus and wanted to serve him in some capacity, I still applied the grid of education and qualifications to ministry opportunities. I hadn't learned yet that God would put me where he wanted me and give me the tools I needed to do *his* job—not my job.

I learned about a local pregnancy care center and decided I was "oh, so qualified" to serve there. After all, I was a nurse, had taught childbirth education classes for years and years, and had personally experienced crisis pregnancy, normal pregnancy, infertility, pregnancy loss, and adoption. And I loved to teach! How much more qualified could I be? And, the director of the program was the woman I had been hired to replace as a Lamaze instructor when we moved to the area. I had it all figured out and enrolled in their volunteer training program.

But I was wrong. Those might have been my plans, but they weren't God's plans. I never did serve in a direct teaching capacity with the center, but I did receive healing for a scarred and devastating past event. That was *his* plan.

And that is only one of many such times I have been somewhere, or doing something, and God has taken me on a detour.

Have you experienced God's detours in your life? Times when you were engaged in some activity or job and you thought you knew the reason, but either another reason or another experience came up?

Are you able to recognize the benefits God's lesson offers compared with your plan?

Do you believe God has lessons for you and a purpose for your life?

Check the following characteristics that apply to you:

___ Self-sufficient
___ Timid
___ Independent
___ Shy
___ Take-charge
___ Control freak
___ Follower
___ Leader
___ Team Player
___ Proud

How can you be more open to the lessons God wants you to learn?

What type of attitude do you think God wants you to have that will be most open to learning the lessons he has for you?

A NEW WAY TO BELIEVE

There are key attributes God seeks as we become more responsive to the lessons he has for us.

Read the following Scripture passages and write what you learn from the passage about accepting instruction from God:

Proverbs 3:5-6
Give a situation in your life you can apply this to:

Psalm 32:8
Give a situation in your life you can apply this to:

Proverbs 14:12
Give a situation in your life you can apply this to:

Proverbs 16:9
Give a situation in your life you can apply this to:

Jeremiah 10:23
Give a situation in your life you can apply this to:

1 Peter 2:21
Give a situation in your life you can apply this to:

How difficult is it for you to get your own agenda out of the way to allow room for God's lessons and plans?

What do you think might help you be more open to what God wants to teach you?

When in doubt, ask for wisdom—it is a prayer God loves to answer! *"If you don't know what you're doing, pray to the Father. He loves to help. You'll get his help, and won't be condescended to when you ask for it"* (James 1:5, MSG).

BELIEVE AND ACT

· Read Isaiah 6:8. What do you think might happen if you
  pray this Scripture?
· Ask God for wisdom daily and the ability to see things
  through his eyes.
· Do you think God's detours will be easier to respond to if
  you view them as opportunities?

ASK THROUGH PRAYER

Dear Lord,

Thanks for the opportunities you give me to learn to live my life
according to your plan. May I be a good student so I don't have too many
detours and can follow your direct route.

Amen.

Day Five:

U-Turns Allowed

THOUGHT FOR THE DAY
When traveling God's roadways, U-turns are always allowed.

WHAT DO YOU BELIEVE?
· God will always give you a fresh start.
· God will give you a fresh start as many times as you need.
· Do you grant others the ability to make U-turns?
· If you wanted to make a U-turn, where would you look for guidance?

WHAT OTHERS MAY THINK
Grace is:
a. A name for a girl.
b. Something you hope you have lots of when your kids are teenagers.
c. A quickie prayer you say before you chow down at meal-time.
d. Unmerited favor from God.

Grace was a concept I was unfamiliar with, certainly as it was applied to me and the mistakes I had made. The concept of a God who loved me, forgave me, and would give me as many chances as I needed to start over was absolutely foreign to me. And the "Christians" I knew didn't do anything to change that.

Why would I want to spend time with God? He couldn't possibly like me, let alone love me—there was no way I was good enough. Fortunately I met grace—and love-filled Christians—it just wasn't until I was well into adulthood and had come to the end of myself.

Do you think God is a God of second, third, and fourth chances? Why or why not?

Have you ever been told by someone, "God will forgive your sins?" If yes, how did that statement make you feel?

Think about what parts of your life you wish you could go back and change. Do you think it's too late, or is it still possible to make a U-turn and have a fresh start?

Are there some decisions you have made that you feel are impossible for God to forgive?

What about forgiving yourself? If God can forgive, can you? Why or why not?

How forgiving are you? Are you willing to let others make U-turns, or do you present some kind of roadblock?

A NEW WAY TO BELIEVE
Read John 1:17. Where does it say grace comes from?

What did grace replace?

Which of the two, grace or law, do Christians you have encountered seem better representatives of?

Write an example of each:

· Grace:

· Law:

How does Romans 5:17 describe the provision of grace God wishes to grant us?

Have you received abundant grace from Christians?

What might abundant grace look like?

If you attend church, how would the people at a Sunday morning service respond to the following individuals showing up for worship?

· A person with several body piercings, some in places you didn't even realize could be pierced

· A person who judging from their odor had been homeless for some time

· A woman who had worked as an exotic dancer

· A person with an ethnic background different from most of the church members

· Someone with a T-shirt advertising beer

· A punk-rock drifter with pink, blue, and purple hair

How welcoming would you be? Would you go up and introduce yourself, or would you stay as far away as possible?

Look up grace in the dictionary. How would grace dictate you respond to each of the individuals above?

What does God say in Psalm 103:12?

What does God say about grace in Ephesians 2:8? Is it a gift or something we earn?

Why are gifts sometimes so difficult for us to accept?

Is it easy or difficult for you to believe that God wishes to bestow the gift of grace on you? Why?

BELIEVE AND ACT
· Think about grace and the effect it has on others. Try to sprinkle with a serving of grace your interactions with others.
· The next time you meet someone who is strikingly different from you, make an effort to extend a gesture of grace. It may be just what they need to make their own U-turn.
· Allow God to bring to your mind someone you need to forgive, and then do so.

ASK THROUGH PRAYER
Father God,

Thank you for mercy, grace, and forgiveness, and give me the ability to always extend them to others instead of shame, blame, and condemnation. Thank you for loving me just as I am and helping me become more like Jesus.

Amen.

I Love Jesus, It's Christians I Don't Get

I didn't grow up in a Christian home. My early church experiences were limited to those I had with my great-grandmother. But as I grew older I did encounter Christians and it often wasn't pretty. Two particular experiences stand out in my mind.

"They'll pay if they mess with my wife," Joe said in a measured tone of voice, practically a hiss. The conversation centered around a perceived wrong directed at his wife at a local facility where she taught part-time. "If they think they can treat my wife like that, they have another think coming. They don't know who they're messing with."

All I could think about was that Joe was a deacon at a church. And I was confused. I knew enough of Jesus to know that love and compassion were priorities. I always thought people who went to church to hear about Jesus would then use him as their example, but there was no love or compassion present in this church representative's voice.

Before that I had witnessed an episode of Christian back-turning (based on Scripture) that just didn't make sense.

A friend's older sister was part of a faith system that mandated marrying within the religion (there would be no unequal yoking, thank you very much) and she was marrying a man who was not a baptized member of her faith, or any faith for that matter. No one went to the wedding except a neighbor. No one from her family showed up.

My early impressions of Christianity had been colored by hurtful experiences my mother and her family had had. *Judgment, gossip,* and *lack of love* were terms used to describe the people of the church and left an indelible impression on both me and my mother. I was inclined to agree with Gandhi, who commented, "I like your Jesus, it's your Christians I don't understand."

But then I met some Christians of a different type, who were influential in my coming into a personal relationship with Christ. These people lived out their faith-loved me, prayed for me, accepted me as I was. Their actions spoke much louder than their words.

God used these people to open the door to my heart. They brought me to a place where I was willing to listen to what they had to share—and accept their love.

There were a number of circumstances God wove together into a life of new possibility for me. There were several friends who, unbeknown to me, had been praying for me. They knew I was hurting and wasn't standing on a rock, but instead was standing in quicksand and sinking fast.

God's timing was perfect. I was ready to unlock the door to my heart, which had been barricaded against God for most of my life. I was ready to get the wax out of my ears and hear God's voice. In Matthew 11:15, Jesus says, "He who has ears, let him hear." And I heard.

In his book *The Unchurched Next Door*, Thom Rainier speaks about the single most important factor influencing people to go to church for the first time. And you know what it is? A personal invitation from someone who cares.

The Holy Spirit used gentle support and a friend's invitation to first bring me to the church I worshipped at for ten years, a day I will never forget. After listening to the sermon I publicly made a commitment to follow Christ in front of the entire congregation during their sharing time.

My friend knew I was hurting and reached out to me in love, not in judgment. She was gentle, yet persistent. She sought to support me, not judge me. She accepted and loved me just the way I was. Period.

When I arrived at the church full of people I had never met, I felt like I had come home. I felt acceptance and love from them. As I listened to the sermon that Sunday morning, I felt as if the pastor were speaking directly to me and there was no one else there.

It seemed like the most natural thing in the world to stand up and say, "My life is in ruins and I need Jesus. Right here, right now, I invite him into my life."

And that was the beginning of my incredible journey of the Christian life.

God and I had been waiting my whole life for that day.

If You Know I'm a Christian, Will you Still Talk to Me?

THOUGHT FOR THE DAY

When you know someone is a Christian does it change how you behave around them? Do you feel differently around them? (More or less comfortable?)

WHAT DO YOU BELIEVE?

- Can you tell someone is a Christian by their actions and how they live, or do they act just like everyone else (or worse)?
- Have you had Christian friends who tried to force you to convert?
- Does or did Christianity seem more like a social club, or duty, than a celebration?
- In your experience have Christians been judgmental, or embracing?

WHAT OTHERS MAY THINK

A Christian is:

a. Someone who reads their Bible every day and goes to church but other than that could have a starring role on LAPD.

b. Someone who preaches a lot and points out your flaws to you all the time while living a hypocritical lifestyle.

c. A Holy Roller.

d. A follower of Christ who loves and serves in his name in a nonjudgmental way.

I have learned that asking someone if she is a Christian is pretty worthless, yet I still do it. What I should do is wait and allow the relationship with the person to grow, and discover the answer to the question that way.

I need to take to heart a friend's comment to me: "If you can't tell I'm a Christian by the way I live my life, then there's a real problem."

Of course there are lots of people who live good lives and are good people and are engaged in good things, but aren't Christians. But is it my job to change that? I would love for them to know Jesus personally and I can play a role, but if I get in their face and proselytize I am only more likely to turn them off. I know, I've experienced it firsthand.

And anyway, even if I ask them if they're Christians, what does the answer mean? Have I given them my definition of what a Christian is, or are they going to answer me based on their beliefs, which may or may not be the same as mine? Does church attendance mean they are Christians? Does slick Scripture-quoting while living a life not in sync count?

My sad observation is that I have met many Christians who damage Christ's reputation through their words and more often actions. I also know many wonderful people who are engaged in lifesaving service who don't want to have anything to do with religion. But I believe there is a huge difference between faith and religion. And I have not been appointed to be their judge; I have, however, been appointed to be their friend.

To me, Christians are ordinary people who are drawn to Christ and seek to become more like him in their life. They examine his teachings and apply them to their lives. So, if you know I'm a Christian, will you still talk to me?

Think about people you know who call themselves Christians. Have they ever shared their faith with you, and if so, how?

What would be the most effective way for Christians to share their faith with you?

Does attending church on Sunday and reading the Bible mean someone is a Christian?

Read the following two vignettes. When you finish, write your impressions.

> Surfing the Web I discovered a site describing an orphanage in a developing country. Mr. Joe left the states with his wife and relocated with the goal of creating a better life for orphaned children. He identified a bene-factor who contributed close to two million dollars to build a state-of-the-art children's home. The facility is beautiful and they are very proud of it.
>
> The children living at the orphanage receive schooling, access to medical care, and several special events, all "provided in Christlike love" (so the glossy brochure boasted). The organization also oversees child sponsorships for several community children living below the poverty level to attend local Christian schools.
>
> Mr. Joe takes every opportunity to share God's Word with everyone, eloquently quoting Bible passages. The organization's mission statement and statement of faith are biblically consistent, and several opportunities to serve as staff, volunteer, or short-term missionaries appeared on the Web site. Mr. Joe and his wife had given

up a comfortable life in the United States to dedicate their life to caring for these kids. Their work is supported by like-minded individuals around the world.

They invite service teams to come down and volunteer, yet there are no set costs available on their Web site.

Cash donations are common, but no financial documents exist for this organization, and sometimes a single child is supported by several sponsors. Long-term volunteers often leave, frustrated by the disconnect between what attracted them to the ministry and what they experience. Mr. Joe traveled to the United States with one of the orphans, a sixteen-year-old girl, and shared a hotel room with her while his wife remained back at the orphanage.

Mr. Joe has fired his board of directors and formed a new nonprofit organization. He lives fully supported by cash donations in a beautiful villa with around-the-clock air conditioning that pulls power away from the local communities, resulting in frequent blackouts.

Another opportunity to serve in the same poor, developing country exists.

It is an opportunity to serve at a local clinic that has also been built through generous support of many benefactors, but their donations are recorded and readily available for review in financial statements and audits.

The clinic grew from one individual's vision and started in her kitchen. When it outgrew the kitchen, it moved to a simple apartment. When it outgrew the apartment it moved to a hotel and finally has its own freestanding building, a simple concrete structure perched on a hillside overlooking the azure seas. It is neat and clean and provides affordable health care to the residents of and visitors to the island.

The needs of the people are met with courtesy and respect and the information is set forth on the clinic's Web site. All people are welcome to serve. Religious affiliation is not a requirement. The leader serves alongside the volunteers in addition to personally delivering medications to community residents and providing transportation to patients who may need more extensive services than the local clinic can provide.

Her home, a simple wood-frame shack surrounded by several other simple homes inhabited by locals, is a type of Grand Central Station to volunteers and visitors from all over. Portable fans that redirect bay breezes are the only tools she uses to cool her home. They are shut off when she leaves the house. She shares her wireless Internet access and her ocean kayaks with all who come to serve. She also has opened her home to a boy whose parents have both been out of the country for a period of time. She has provided a bed to sleep in, food to eat, and love to nourish his soul.

Does one organization strike you as "more Christian" than the other? Why or why not?

What aspects of either organization appeal to you?

Does anything turn you off?

A NEW WAY TO BELIEVE

Rather than look at people, who by their nature are flawed and far from perfect, look at the person of Jesus to discover who he is and what attributes describe him best. Jesus is the role model for Christians.

Read Matthew 11:29 (we have read this passage before). How does Jesus describe himself?

Think about these two key attributes. Do you personally know a Christian who exemplifies and models these characteristics?

Can you use these two attributes to describe yourself? What can you do to help make that possible?

Jesus cared about people and conversed with them. Do the Christians you know care about people and build relationships with them, or do they shy away?

Did Jesus hang out with "sinners"? (See Matthew 9:9-13; John 4:1-26)

Do you think of Christians today as hanging out with similar types?

I recently learned of a church leader who frequently holds leadership meetings with his team at a local bar. What is your reaction?

BELIEVE AND ACT
- What will I say if someone asks me if I am a Christian?
- What one change can I make today that will show others I am a follower of Christ?
- Do you believe that actions speak louder than words, and if so, is this a relevant way to share one's faith?

ASK THROUGH PRAYER
Jesus,
Help me love with your love. Help me see others with your eyes. Help others know I am a Christian by my love.
Amen.

DAY TWO:

ARE *You* SO FAR TO THE RIGHT THAT *You're* *in* LEFT FIELD?

THOUGHT FOR THE DAY

Keep in mind that Jesus didn't polarize himself, and communicated with everyone from the religious leaders of the day to the outcasts.

WHAT DO YOU BELIEVE?

- Do you tend to categorize Christians by their political affiliation?
- Is there a "one-size-fits-all" label for Christians?
- What kinds of issues do the Christians you know care about?
- Would you place Jesus on the political "right" or on the "left?"

WHAT OTHERS MAY THINK

Tolerance is:

a. When your antibiotic no longer works to knock out your staph infection.

b. When you think you have "arrived" because you keep inappropriate comments to yourself.
c. What my older sister has for her younger sister when she doesn't whack her back after being poked at.
d. Extending grace to others.

Judgment is:
a. What is levied against you when you don't pay your taxes.
b. What is going to happen when the battle of Armageddon comes.
c. The attitude most of the Christians I encountered growing up had down to an art form.
d. What is reserved for God to pass and is not up to humans to dish out.

One of the many things that impress me about Jesus is that he interacted with all kinds of people, from the "sinners" of the day to the Pharisees, who were the Jewish religious leaders and keepers of the law.

One story illustrates his interaction with both at the same gathering (Luke 7:36-50). Following is a synopsis:

Jesus is invited by one of the Pharisees to dinner, so he goes to this guy's house and reclines at the table. While he is there, a "woman who had lived a sinful life" (it doesn't tell us specifically what her sins were) learns Jesus is there and goes over to the Pharisee's house. She brings an alabaster jar with perfume and stands behind Jesus and weeps. She then washes his feet, as was customary in that day when visitors arrived, to cleanse the dust from their feet, but she does it with her tears. The Pharisee immediately notices and thinks to himself that if Jesus is the prophet he says he is, he would know she was a sinner and wouldn't let her touch him. But Jesus knows what the Pharisees are thinking and uses the experience as a teaching point, something he did frequently.

In Luke 7:41-43, what example did Jesus use to illustrate the lesson he wanted to teach the Pharisee?

In verses 44 through 46, what did the "sinful" woman do that the Pharisee did not?

What did Jesus do in verse 48?

What quality did the woman have that the Pharisees lacked?

Have you met Christians who are like the Pharisee? How about like the sinful woman?

What lesson(s) can you learn from the Pharisee?

What lesson(s) can you learn from the sinful woman?

Read Ephesians 4:2-3. How does it say we should relate to each other?

A NEW WAY TO BELIEVE
How would your faith life be different if we followed the guidance offered in Ephesians 4:2-3?

Do you see a unity of peace among Christians?

What can you do to keep or promote the "bond of peace?"

I love a statement a friend of mine made. It serves as a powerful reminder how we, as imperfect human beings, have distorted the church. (Remember, the church is the body of Christ.) She said, "God made the church, people made denominations." Do you think denominations end up unifying Christians or do they end up being more divisive?

What does Romans 15:5 say?

Whom are we instructed to follow to gain the spirit of unity?

Galatians 5:22-23 tells the attributes of the "fruit of the Spirit."
List them here: Now tell how you may manifest them in your life:

1._____   _____
2._____   _____
3._____   _____
4._____   _____
5._____   _____
6._____   _____
7._____   _____
8._____   _____
9._____   _____

Now look back to Galatians 5:19-21, which list attributes of the sinful nature, or nature contrary to what pleases God. List them here, highlighting each one you have experienced.

Do you get angry (not just upset—real fits of rage)? I do. How does James 1:19 instruct us to avoid anger?

Do you envy? What about your neighbor's newer, bigger, nicer house with the big-screen TV and the stainless steel appliances and granite countertops? What does Proverbs 14:30 tell us envy will do? What does 1 Timothy 6:8 tell us to do?

Are you given to selfish ambition? Are there times you do things because of what's in it for you, rather than to be of service to others? (If I am honest, I readily admit there have been (and still are) times I am prone to this.) What does Paul write about selfish ambition in Philippians 2:3?

BELIEVE AND ACT
- Select one attribute of the "fruit of the spirit" (from Galatians 5:21-22) to focus on. Pray that you may demonstrate more of this fruit to others on a daily basis.
- What can you do on a regular basis to live in unity with other Christians?
- In what area can you work to become more tolerant and less judgmental?

ASK THROUGH PRAYER
Dear God,

Please help me live a balanced life and be thankful for what I have, realizing that most of my "needs" are really "wants." Help people know I love you, as demonstrated by a life of love, joy, peace, patience, kindness, goodness, faithfulness, gentleness, and self-control. I know I can't even come close to doing this myself, so please help me grow little by little in these areas. Thank you.

Amen.

Day THRee:

WHY Do THey Always Sound as If THey're Preaching?

THOUGHT FOR THE DAY

As Christians become more involved in their church and hang out with their Christian friends more and more, they sometimes seem to speak a new language that is hard to understand and sounds preachy.

WHAT DO YOU BELIEVE?

- If/when you go to church, can you understand the message or is it sometimes in the foreign language of *Christianese?*
- Do you know Christians who use words and phrases you don't understand? How about Christians who speak like "normal" people?

WHAT OTHERS MAY THINK

Christianese is:

a. A language reserved for those who attend church and is full of thee's and thou's.

b. A foreign language reserved for everyone better than you.

c. Language that serves to alienate those outside the church and make them feel so uncomfortable they won't want to come in.

d. Christian phrases churchgoers (including believers) pick up and use without realizing that people without a church background may not understand.

At my first church I worked alongside people who care about missions and outreach. I write a monthly newsletter called *Missions Musings*. The newsletter communicated different initiatives and opportunities we have that people can become involved with. It's a way to communicate what's happening to those who pick it up, whether they attend our church or not.

I run what I've written past a couple of people before we copy it, and last month I received some very valuable feedback that made my heart sink.

The observation was that I had written it as an "insider" to "insiders." I had failed to define terms that those not attending our church would not understand. I had fallen prey to the insidious disease of *Christianspeak*: communicating in an exclusive language. It wasn't my intent, yet it had happened.

Have there been times you went to church and didn't understand a word the pastor was saying? Can you describe a specific example?

I recall that when I first started attending church the pastor kept talking about "saints." And it wasn't a Catholic church, so I really had no idea whom he was talking about. But that word popped up all the time; "the saints this" and "the saints that." I was clueless. I still don't remember when I finally realized that "the saints" referred to everyday, ordinary people like me and you who are followers of Jesus.

The apostle Paul, a key New Testament writer and Pharisee turned missionary, uses the term throughout the New Testament when referring to fellow followers of Jesus. I do remember the first time I learned about the apostle Paul. A person wrote a note to me identifying Paul and telling me he had previously been known as Saul of Tarsus. I learned more about the apostle Paul that day from my mail lady who was a Christian than I had from anyone else I had ever heard talk about him.

Do people make assumptions that you understand them when they start speaking Christianese? Or do they not care?

Are there phrases you have heard in church or from Christians that strike you as weird or offensive?

Do you feel comfortable asking them to pause and explain what the heck they're talking about, or do you simply hope they will be quiet?

Do you know about the Old Testament and the New Testament? Do you know what language(s) each was originally written in?

I appreciate so much the fact that our pastor will often mention where specific books of the Bible are located for those who wish to follow along, but I also appreciate the fact that my church projects on a screen the Scriptures referred to in the message.

A NEW WAY TO BELIEVE

In his book *They Like Jesus, but Not the Church*, Dan Kimball talks about what happens to people over time after they become Christians. He talks about "the transformation from Excited Missionary into Citizen of the Bubble." It is very true, and in my opinion very sad.

Basically, when we first become followers of Christ, we are excited (and I was a bit obnoxious). We want to share what is, and I remember wanting to tell everyone about Jesus. I looked at sharing Jesus as if sharing a sumptuous (to my palate, anyway) meal with friends who weren't the least bit hungry.

"Hey, I've got this great stuff I'd love you to try," I'd say.

"No, thanks," they'd answer.

"No, no, really, here, I insist, have some!" I'd push, an agitated edge working its way into my voice.

"No, really-I'm not hung- . . ."

Not letting them even finish their sentence I would thrust the afore-mentioned sumptuous meal in their face like the tradition of the bride and groom shoving wedding cake in each other's face.

Then many new Christians start to go to church (and Bible studies, and Sunday school, and small group) and volunteer for every ministry under the sun and soon settle very comfortably into church life and start to lose touch with old friends.

Then they become part of what Kimball refers to as the "Christian Bubble." He writes, "We get more excited about going overseas to the mission field on summer trips than about the mission field we live in every day."

Kimball continues, "We start to see evangelism as inviting people to go to a church, where the pastor will do the evangelizing and explain Christianity, instead of spending time with people and talking with them and being the church to them."

And then after several years as "citizens of the bubble" we moan and groan about the awful world out there and lock ourselves into our church world.

We are instructed to "not conform . . . to the pattern of this world" (Romans 12:2), yet we live in the world. If we are going to care about people, which is what Jesus did, then we need to understand what's going on in the world and in our culture without following the world and our culture.

We are to hold our Bibles in one hand and our newspapers in the other.

How can you make sure you don't become enclosed in the Christian Bubble?

Do you know people who seem to be a part of the Christian Bubble? How might you encourage them to burst the bubble?

BELIEVE AND ACT

· Continue to engage in relationships with others from all areas of life.

- Become engaged in your community. How can you make a difference?
- Don't be shy about pointing it out to someone else if they start blabbering in Christianese and you don't understand a word they're saying.
- If you are a follower of Christ, offer to mentor someone else as they seek to find out more about Jesus. In Christianese we have a word for this, it is called "discipling" or "discipleship."

ASK THROUGH PRAYER

Lord,

Thanks for loving me right here right now just as I am, even if I don't understand a word they are saying. Help me serve you in a way that is matched with my abilities and where I am spiritually. If I need to be bold, gentle, quiet, or enthusiastic, give me the courage to do so.

Amen.

DAY FOUR:

WITH FRIENDS LIKE THEM, WHO NEEDS ENEMIES?

THOUGHT FOR THE DAY

Aside from loving the Lord our God with all our hearts and souls, we are commanded to love our neighbors as ourselves.

WHAT DO YOU BELIEVE?

· Do you think the Ten Commandments apply to us today as much as they did to the Israelites when they were written?
· What does it look like to love your neighbor?
· Have there been times you have felt more like an enemy than a friend to a Christian?
· Where does the ability to truly love come from?

WHAT OTHERS MAY THINK

Love is:
a. What cootie shots protect third grade girls and boys from. gave cooties against coming down with in third and fourth grade.
b. That overpowering physical attraction between guys and gals, young and not so young.

c. An overused word in song lyrics.
d. What God personifies.

There is a hymn that proclaims, "They will know we are Christians by our love." Is love the first word that comes to mind when you think of Christians? If not, what is?

Have you experienced love from Christians? If so, how?

Was something expected in return or was it really an unconditional, no-strings-attached love?

How easy or hard is it to love unconditionally?

__ Impossible
__ Very difficult
__ Difficult
__ Fairly easy
__ Really easy
__ Automatic

Do you know people who seem to do a pretty good job at this?

What strikes you about them? Do they tend to put their needs or the needs of others first?

Do you think it comes automatically for them or is it a struggle?

What do you think helps them model love?

What are some different ways of modeling love to others? This can be as simple as showing someone else you care. Write your thoughts here:

Do you think recognition for all the good things you are doing and the love you are sharing is necessary? Is announcing them to the world a good idea?

A NEW WAY TO BELIEVE

The essence of God is love. Read 1 John 4:16. What does it say to you?

Galatians 5:14 states, "The entire law [how we are to live] is summed up in a single command," and goes on to tell what that command is. What is it?

What attributes of love are written in 1 Corinthians 13:4-6?

Verse 7 states that love always does what?

What does love never do (verse 8)?

What can you do to share God's love with others, using actions that model the attributes above?

Think about your relationship with those closest to you. Does your love demonstrate those attributes?

BELIEVE AND ACT

· The next time you are tempted to ignore someone and a need you know exists, make an effort instead to meet the need.
· Start to think about this: If each person in the world would just make a conscious choice to make a difference in one other person's life, the world would be a better place.
· Start viewing the world as your neighborhood.

ASK THROUGH PRAYER

Lord,

Help me see others with your eyes, hear their voices with your ears, and respond to their needs with your compassion. In this way may I be your hands and feet on Earth.

Amen.

DAY FIVE:

You're a Sinner Going to Hell, But Have I Told You Lately that I Love You?

THOUGHT FOR THE DAY

How we share our faith is at least as important as, if not more important than, what we say.

WHAT DO YOU BELIEVE?

· Does it matter how faith is shared?
· How have others shared their faith with you? Was it effective or ineffective?
· If someone is a Christian, do they have to share their faith with words?
· Do you think faith-sharing is a one-shot deal?

WHAT OTHERS MAY THINK

An evangelist is:
a. Christianity's hypocritical poster child, as seen on TV.

b. Someone who will shove their beliefs down your throat.

c. The guy on the street corner who hands out pamphlets called tracts, or the missionary who goes to a foreign country and leads thousands of people in a simple prayer they don't understand.

d. One who shares the gospel, the good news of Christ, through words and works.

When someone uses the word *evangelist*, what image comes to mind?

I was recently in New York City and passed through a street fair on Sixth Avenue. There among the T-shirt and handbag vendors were two guys serving as street evangelists. One was holding a sign on which were emblazoned the words, "Do you know where you are spending eternity? Are you going to hell?"

It looked like a picket sign, and I suppose it was: a sign protesting the sorry state of so many lost and damned souls. While he held the sign and pumped it up and down, his buddy thrust tracts proclaiming man's one-way ticket to hell to anyone who came within arm's reach.

Another type of evangelism that has been common over the years has been the door-to-door evangelist. These people usually travel in tandem. They are not easily dissuaded and typically arrive when I am in the middle of supervising homework or cooking dinner. When they ask if they can just share (debate) for a couple of minutes, they don't take no for an answer very well. One foot is usually in the door before I have an opportunity to respond. When I say I know Jesus, it just invites more persistence. I don't want to be rude, but mutual respect appears to be lacking in the conversation. I do not respond well to people banging on my door at busy times of day. Then again maybe they don't know Jesus and I can tell them about him!

A style of sharing referred to as friendship evangelism is one that appears to be gaining momentum. This makes sense to me. Get to know the person, take the time to build a relationship, and demonstrate the no-strings-attached service and love that Christ would share. A friend of mine was engaged in this kind of faith-sharing with the homeless population in San Francisco. Her stories are inspiring.

You can engage in this kind of faith-sharing with your neighbors. Get to know them. Respond to their needs. Be a good friend and when invited, or when the opportunity arises, gently share bits and pieces of your faith.

The drawback? It takes time. Isn't it much easier to hand out tracts and hope someone will respond? Or go door to door and hope you can push your way in? Or even go on a mission trip to a foreign country and lead a mass prayer of salvation whether or not the audience even really understands?

Do you agree with the following statement: "Evangelism is simply sharing your faith with others in a variety of ways"? Why or why not?

What different evangelistic methods have you experienced?

Which was (were) most helpful to you?

Which was (were) least helpful?

What is the most helpful thing Christians could do to help you understand their beliefs?

What is the most hurtful thing you have experienced from a Christian?

Do you think prayer can be a form of evangelism? Why or why not?

Do you think kids can be evangelists? Why or why not?

What kinds of activities can kids engage in that may be forms of evangelism?

Two words typically associated with evangelism are witness and sinner. What do these words mean to you?

If you think of sin as "separation from God," does that leave a more palatable impression?

What about witness? Being a witness is really nothing more than sharing your story of how God is working in your life. Another word for this is "testimony." So why don't we just share our stories without applying labels?

A NEW WAY TO BELIEVE

Jesus loved to tell stories; in fact, he did much of his teaching through the use of parables (illustrations). The first four books of the New Testament, the Gospels (Matthew, Mark, Luke, and John), are full of examples of Jesus' parables.

Do you think the use of stories is an effective teaching tool? When we see ourselves in a story or it is told in terms familiar to us, is it easier to understand?

What does James 1:22 say?

Is listening to or reading the word of God enough? If not, what else is required?

What does James 1:27 say God accepts as pure and faultless religion?

Are people who serve in orphanages or look after widows evangelists? Why or why not?

I recently had a conversation with someone who has been turned off by religion. It was illuminating and served to confirm some impressions I have developed over time: that actions speak louder than words; referring to me to my face as a sinner will not enamor me to you or your God; force-feeding your beliefs to me will turn me off; but simple yet consistent service will make an impression.

This individual spoke about two individuals who had made an indelible impression on him. One was a missionary who simply asked if he could pray for him and wrote his name down on a piece of paper and then left it at that. The other was a woman who has dedicated her life to making access to improved health care and basic services like clean water a reality for people in the community in which she lives. He commented that he very much respected and appreciated the fact that she just simply served without adding a bunch of religious hype to what she was doing. And he noted she has done more good than many of the so-called religious missionaries. But he knows she loves Jesus; he simply respects that she doesn't cram that love down his throat.

Contrast these experiences with an interaction I had with a prominent evangelist. I didn't know who he was at the time, but figured he must be someone important by the way people were hovering. We were both guests invited to share parts of our stories with a TV audience. He didn't give me the time of day, wore a smile on his face that I thought might have been botoxed in place, and was catered to by the studio staff. In fact he had another commitment, so our time slots were flip-flopped without so much as a "thank you" (and on top of it he overran his allotted time).

When I learned who he was, I was interested in his perspective on a couple of questions, and hoped to have a short conversation with him. It was curt, to the point, and not very edifying. Soon after our meeting a story broke revealing several inconsistencies between what he practiced and what he preached.

I couldn't help but think of the lyrics of the Michael W. Smith song *Kentucky Rose*: "He practiced what he preached, imagine that." Unfortunately it appears that the "imagine that" part is alive and well in the inconsistent actions of even prominent representatives of the faith.

What is your response to this story?

Yes, we are all human and make mistakes (we're sinners), but humility and repentance were definitely missing and that made me sad. How important is it to "practice what we preach?"

If evangelism is sharing your faith in Christ, then what are some effective, inoffensive ways you can do that?

Do you believe evangelism is something everyone can do, or is it limited to pastors and missionaries?

If you are asked why you are doing what you are doing, and are doing it because of love for and as service to Christ, are you prepared with a gentle way of sharing that with others? See 1 Peter 3:15.

What does Matthew 28:19 say?

BELIEVE AND ACT

· How would your relationship with Jesus change if you took your role as an evangelist seriously?
· How can you share the gospel through your actions?
· Are you intrigued by "friendship evangelism"?

ASK THROUGH PRAYER

Dear God,

Help me be a friend to others, always sharing with them the love you have for me, serving as your hands and feet. Help me become and then remain humble, steadfast, and hardworking in my service to you and to others.

Amen.

week Five:

I'd Rather Have a Maid than Be a Servant

Whenever I thought about church (which for many years was not much), it was definitely all about me. How could church serve me? What could I get out of it? The concept Rick Warren addresses in *The Purpose-Driven Life*, the "It's not about you" philosophy, was totally absent.

Unfortunately the "It's all about me" attitude is still alive and well, even among church members and churchgoers. And I have to admit, there are still many times I look for what I can get out of church. Did the sermon "speak" to me? Were my spiritual needs met? Don't get me wrong, spiritual growth is important, and often takes place in the context of Sunday morning services. But it was a while before I realized there was much more to church than showing up on Sundays and that Christian service to God and to those around us was necessary for the church to function as Christ intended.

When I was still in the "What can I get out of it?" mindset, I would try to figure out how different church programs could cater to me. At the beginning of the summer, I would grab a calendar and plot out a summer's worth of Vacation Bible School (VBS) activities. If I planned it right, I could have my young children enrolled in a VBS each week of the summer.

I became giddy with excitement! I would have two to three hours of free child care and activities for my kids to engage in, while I heaved a huge parental sigh of relief and took a load off. Some VBS's were in the morning, others in the evening, but the best were those that were three hours long and were close to home. It was so about me.

I imagined uninterrupted scrapbooking sessions and quiet dinners with just my husband. Not once did I give a thought to the army of volunteers it took to provide the experience, or the spiritual blessings my kids would receive.

I was taking advantage of the service of others, who had it right. I wanted a maid (to be waited on) and had no interest (or thought of) being a servant.

That attitude doesn't change overnight. I love Jesus passionately. But there are many days I would still rather have a maid than be a servant. I have, however, learned a thing or two along the way.

It isn't all about me. It is all about sharing the love of Christ with others. Fortunately we are blessed with different gifts and talents that suit us and are very effective when used to serve others. We need to be open and alert to the opportunity to talk when we are asked about why we serve.

I will never be the best choice to lead a group of eight-year-old boys with attention-deficit disorder in Sunday school or VBS; but teach an adult Sunday school class on an area I am passionate about? Or reach out to hurting women with whom I can identify in a real and transparent "I don't have it all together" way? Now that's exciting to me! (But won't be to everyone.)

Thankfully we each have our unique gifts and purpose and when we understand it is about how we can serve, then we can cancel the maid service.

Day One:

Stop the Whining and Just Do It

THOUGHT FOR THE DAY

Keep in mind that Christian service isn't lip service, it's sacrifice.

WHAT DO YOU BELIEVE?

· Do you equate service with sacrifice?
· Do Christians embrace the opportunity to serve, or do you think some would rather write a check?
· What are some barriers to service?

WHAT OTHERS MAY THINK

Service is:

a. What I expect when I eat at a five-star restaurant.
b. What I take my car in for at regular intervals so it doesn't break down.
c. What I used to call church.
d. A way of life that involves sacrifice, which demonstrates, without using words, my commitment to Christ.

I recently overheard a conversation between two acquaintances who reflected my long-held (but now long-gone) feelings about church attendance, membership, and service.

The gist of the conversation was that Friend A had switched churches because she and her family were no longer "getting anything out of" the church they had been going to and the priest was driving them nuts. So they started attending a different church down the street. The new church was a very nice church with a kid-friendly environment for their four-year-old daughter, something very important to them.

But the next sentence caught me off guard. It struck me as backward. *"Yeah, we just got baptized, but when they asked us if we wanted to become members, we said, 'No, we are too busy.'"*

Yet I could identify with it. Just let me be "in" but don't ask me to volunteer my time.

Which do you think is the more "serious" commitment: membership or baptism?

Do you think baptism signifies a commitment to God that leads to service or is simply a ticket to heaven?

Do you think church membership means you will be expected to share your time and money? If so, what is your reaction?

What if you attend church on a regular basis and have been baptized but aren't a member. Does that let you off the service hook? Why or why not?

Is service a pain or a privilege? Why?

Does your answer change if you define church as followers of Christ rather than members of a particular denomination?

Do you think Christian service is only designed for retirees, stay-at-home parents, and other people you perceive to have "extra" time, or is it something everyone who attends regularly needs to become involved in?

When it comes to service, my experience is that people are reluctant to get involved. What are some of the reasons you may choose not to get involved in serving at church? Check all that apply:

___ I'm too busy.
___ I'm not qualified.
___ It's not a priority to me.
___ I'm tired.
___ God won't miss me.
___ There aren't any ministry opportunities that interest me.
___ I would rather write a check.

Now take another look at the list. What do they all have in common?

Read Philippians 2:4. How often do we put the needs of others first? How often do we put the needs of the church ahead of what we can get out of it?

A NEW WAY TO BELIEVE

Service generally requires sacrifice. If we are giving our time and it is something we would do anyway, it's not too much of a sacrifice. If we are donating items to help others, it's not much of a sacrifice if the next option is the dumpster.

I heard a speaker address this issue. Boy, did this guy have passion!

He said, "I came to the United States a few years ago from Honduras. I didn't have too many belongings, but I had enough to manage." He paused and looked around the room, allowing us to absorb this truth. He had enough to manage. Did I have enough to manage? I realized I had way more than enough to manage.

He continued, "There were many well-meaning people who wanted to give me things to make my life easier, but let me tell you something, the lime green prom tux that has been in the back of your closet since 1974 will not make my life easier. I don't want it any more than you do."

That hit me hard. How many times had I thought I was giving or serving, but it didn't involve any sacrifice on my part—just a way of disposing of some unwanted item, or volunteering because of some personal agenda? Isn't this selfish ambition?

Back to sacrificial service. What does Romans 12:1 say?

What are we supposed to offer? Why?

What do you think is meant by "God's mercy"? What did God do for us? (Hint: The answer is in John 3:16.)

God sacrificed his son for us by allowing him to be crucified, a horrible act of brutality. Now if that's not sacrifice, I don't know what is.

We don't need to engage in such extreme sacrifice, but service is how we express our love to God for what he has done for us. It's pretty insulting to give him our leftovers and saving the best for ourselves.

Back to Romans 12:1. What is "offering your bodies as a living sacrifice" referred to as?

Did you realize before now how pleasing this is to God?

What are some ways you can start serving today?

Are there ways you can serve at your church?

Service doesn't have to be dramatic; it can be a simple act.

BELIEVE AND ACT

- Think of a time when you really experienced "It's more blessed to give than receive." What were some of the characteristics that made giving or serving special?

· List three ways you can incorporate service into your daily
   and weekly routine.
· Do you think giving money is easier than giving time?
· Has there ever been a time your service was sacrificial?

ASK THROUGH PRAYER
Jesus,

Thank you for teaching me about love and sacrifice. Help me become more like you and look for opportunities to serve you by loving others and meeting their needs every day. Help me move from wanting a maid to becoming a servant.

Amen.

Day Two:

I Never Knew There Was More Than One Martha

THOUGHT FOR THE DAY

The original Martha of the hospitality world is not Martha Stewart, but Martha, sister of Lazarus and friend of Jesus. She also had a sister named Mary. The two sisters can teach us a lot about hospitality. In fact, we learn the true message of hospitality not from Martha Stewart or her Biblical counterpart, but from Mary. While Martha rushed around cooking, cleaning, and getting ready, yet ignored her guest Jesus, Mary sat at his feet, placing a higher priority on relating to him than taking care of the house and meal.

WHAT DO YOU BELIEVE?

- Is it more important to have a clean home or a clean heart?
- Think of people you know who have a servant's heart. What qualities do they have?
- Is it more welcoming to guests to be bustling around getting the house perfect and the meal ready, or to sit and actively engage them in conversation, listening to what they have to share?
- Which type of hospitality do you practice more often?

WHAT OTHERS MAY THINK

Hospitality is:

a. The suite I always wanted to go to but can't because I don't belong.

b. A gift I never thought I had because I couldn't figure out where the different spoons and forks belonged.

c. A gift I don't want to have because it might mean too many overnight guests.

d. A gift that involves sharing of self and welcoming others regardless of how big (or small) your home is. What matters is how big your heart is.

For many years I placed a neat, clean house at the top of my priority list. Picking up the toys was more important than playing with them. Lining the books up on the shelf was more important than reading them to my children. I loved the feeling of control that came with things put away in their place.

Thankfully I have become more balanced in my neat-freak approach to life over the years. I still crave order and organization—I think more clearly when things are in order. But I am learning to place a higher priority on relationships than on how my house looks.

I remember a time when a friend stopped by my home to return a book. It was around suppertime and my daughters both had friends over. They were all hungry and I was trying to get them dinner while supervising the last little bit of homework. The phone kept ringing, the cat had just eaten grass and thrown up, and one of the friends finished his homework and decided to put the TV on, adding to the chaos. By this time I had blown up several hot dogs in the microwave (our dog came out the big winner on that one) and decided spaghetti might be a better bet.

Then the doorbell rang.

"Oh, Kathy," my friend Karen said, "I hope you don't mind. I'm just waiting for my son to be done with basketball practice, and wanted to return this book to you."

Spaghetti spoon in hand, I ushered her into my house, tripping over a shoe in the process. "Come in, come in," I said.

She looked at me not sure if I was sincere but when I insisted with a smile and a shrug, she came in. We chatted for a couple of minutes while

I scooped the spaghetti out of the pot before it burned, and pleaded with the kids to turn off the TV.

As soon as I got the spaghetti under control I sat down with her for a few minutes to catch up. I didn't think anything of it, but it made a huge impression on her.

Several weeks later I ran into Karen at the grocery store. "Do you remember that evening I came over to return the book?" she asked.

I nodded.

"Well," she continued, "I have to tell you how welcome you made me feel."

I must have looked shocked as she nodded her head emphatically.

"You really made me feel welcome. You had kids over, were obviously trying to get them dinner, and I just appeared, and you invited me into your home."

She paused, reflecting on the memory for a moment, and then continued, "I could never do that. My house has to be perfectly in order before I let anyone in."

My simple gesture had made a huge impression.

Can you remember a similar time in your life when you placed interaction with a person above what your house looked like?

On a scale from 1 to 10, rate how strongly you agree with the following statements.
1 = strongly agree, 10 = strongly disagree.

__ I answer my e-mails before I answer my kids' questions.
__ I can't invite anyone inside my house unless it is spotless.
__ I hate it when people show up without calling first.
__ I will drop everything to have coffee with a friend.
__ I insist people who visit my house take their shoes off.
__ When I plan my weekend I pay as much attention to what my kids want to do as I do to my own agenda.

What did this exercise reveal to you? Does this surprise you?

Will you change anything based on your answers to the questions above?

Is there someone you admire who can serve as a role model?

A NEW WAY TO BELIEVE

Read the story of Martha and Mary in Luke 10:38-42.

· What positive attributes does Martha have?

· What positive attributes does Mary have?

· Are you more like Martha or Mary?

· Who would Jesus like us to be more like and why?

· What is it Mary did that was of such value to Christ?

· What kind of hospitality does Jesus value?

Look up Luke 14:12-14. Whom does Jesus say we should invite as dinner guests?

How could you do this?

What kind of attitude should we have when we offer hospitality? See 1 Peter 4:9.

BELIEVE AND ACT

· List three ways you can be a "Mary" to your friends:

1.

2.

3.

· Is there a way you can make Christlike hospitality a tradition in your family?

· Identify one Martha-like quality you have and commit to replacing it with a Mary-like quality over the next month.

ASK THROUGH PRAYER

Thank you, Jesus, for teaching me what real hospitality is. Thank you for teaching me I don't need to be like Martha (either one). Help me value the simple things in life.

Amen.

DAY THREE:

Being *a* Blessing Is Nothing to Sneeze At

THOUGHT FOR THE DAY

Blessings come in many different shapes and sizes and can easily be missed.

WHAT DO YOU BELIEVE?

· Are blessings available to everyone? If so, why do some people miss them?
· Do you believe in coincidences, or do you believe that everything happens for a reason?
· Can God use you to bless someone?
· Are blessings personalized?

WHAT OTHERS MAY THINK

Bless You is:
a. What you say when someone sneezes.
b. What you coyly remark when someone gives you their seat on a crowded bus.
c. Just another way of saying thank you.
d. A desire to release God's favor.

My mother returned to work outside the home when I was eight and in third grade. This was in the late 1960s and in retrospect her employers, the American Bible Society, were way, way ahead of their time. They granted her the ultimate in flextime. They allowed her to arrange her work schedule around my school calendar. She worked from nine to three the days I was in school and had off all holidays, summers, and days I was home sick.

My mother returned to work full-time when I was in high school and was given credit for all her years of part-time work toward vacation time accrual and health and life insurance benefits.

In addition, since her retirement, she has had full medical and dental benefits, not only for herself but for my dad as well. Coincidence or blessing?

My mom still thinks it is simply a stroke of good fortune, but I gently point out to her that her benefits are a blessing and not mere coincidence. Her employer was a Christian organization who lived out Christian values and blessed their employees through, among other things, their benefits package.

But it is all in your perspective. I have never been one to believe in coincidences; I have always believed things happen for a reason. The missing link for me was how it all played out as part of God's plan.

Do you believe that things generally happen for a reason, or are coincidental?

Think of a time when something amazing happened to you that was just too wild to be a coincidence. What was it?

Why do you think you had this experience?

What was the blessing that came from this experience?

List times when you have been blessed:

· With encouragement:

· With friendship:

· Financially:

· With a second chance:

· With the gift of time:

· With a need being met in a totally unexpected way:

· When you didn't deserve it:

· In a way that was specifically designed to be meaningful just for you:

What about blessing others? Name times you have been a blessing (a source of joy, encouragement, hope, or some other gift) to someone else:

Do you think God uses you to bless others? Why or why not?

Do you think God wants to bless you? Why or why not?

A NEW WAY TO BELIEVE

Sometimes God's blessings are subtle. I have noticed that many times they are also related to prayer and asking for the blessing. The verses in Matthew indicate it's okay to ask. In fact, we often miss out on blessings because we don't ask (see James 4:2).

And how beautifully and personally God answers those prayers with blessings designed just for us. For me the blessing of encouragement comes from seeing brilliant rays of sunshine breaking through the clouds. It is as if God is saying directly to me, "It's okay. I am the light of the world, and I am extending that light and everything it represents directly to you." But those rays of sunshine may not be the personalized signature for someone else.

What is God's personalized message of hope for you?

God also sometimes speaks to us in upside-down ways. The Scripture passage known as the Beatitudes describes blessings in para-doxical (upside-down) ways. It flies in the face of how we live and think in the modern world, but give this a try—you will be blessed! And by this I mean you will discover something new about yourself.

Look up Matthew 5:3-11 in the New International Version and *The Message*. Compare the two side by side. (If you have Internet access, remember www.biblegateway.com.)

Think about a time when you felt each of the following and reflect upon what you discovered about yourself.

· Felt poor in spirit. What was the discovery?

· Mourned. How were you comforted, and what was the discovery?

· Felt meek. What was the discovery?
· Sought righteousness? What was the discovery?

· Were merciful. What was the discovery?

· Were pure in heart. What was the discovery?

· Served as a peacemaker. What was the discovery?

· Suffered persecution. What was the discovery?

BELIEVE AND ACT
· Contemplate a way you can be a blessing to someone else this week. It can be simple. Learn to listen for that still, small voice that prompts you with suggestions how to do this, and then follow through.

· Pick one of the character qualities listed in the Beatitudes and develop it as a habit, but be patient with yourself. It will take lots of repetition and won't happen overnight. Remember, it can take up to twenty-eight days to develop a new habit.
· Think of blessings as a way you can surprise people by putting their needs before your own.

ASK THROUGH PRAYER

Dear God,

Thank you so much for wanting to be my friend and wanting to bless me. Help me delight in your ways and yield myself to be used by you as a blessing to others.

Amen.

DAY FOUR:

Mission Impossible: Please Don't Send Me to Africa

THOUGHT FOR THE DAY
The mission field is just as available across the street as around the world.

WHAT DO YOU BELIEVE?
· When someone talks about missions, what comes to mind?
· Do you think of outreach as the same as missions?
· Is there a mission field available to you? What is it?
· Can kids serve as missionaries?

WHAT OTHERS MAY THINK
Missionary is:
a. Someone who goes to Africa to toil endlessly.
b. An older, single woman, similar to a librarian, with whom I have nothing in common.
c. A style of furniture.
d. Every follower of Christ who shares her love and words with others regardless of where it is.

For many years both before and after I started learning about and using Jesus as the teacher and role model in my life, I had a preconceived notion of missionaries and what they looked like.

My impression was that they were usually older singles or couples (never children) who went to serve in faraway places, and their service amounted to telling (not showing) the natives about Christ, and if they didn't get to know him the future was bleak. I imagined their speech to be similar to that of the teachers in the Charlie Brown cartoons—a nasal, unintelligible droning *ad infinitum*.

Fortunately, I couldn't have been more mistaken.

Over time I came to realize we are all missionaries, followers of Jesus who are called to share him with everyone around us, whether across the street or around the world, through good works and good words.

It dawned on me that outreach and missions really describe the same activities and goals: to introduce or broaden others' relationships with Christ. The only difference is location: one is local (outreach) and the other is global (missions).

All kinds of opportunities exist for us to serve as missionaries—those who share the love of Christ with others—and you need look no farther than your own neighborhood to begin.

Is this a new way for you to think about missionaries? In what way?

Do you consider yourself a missionary?

Look up disciple in the dictionary. What is the definition?

According to Matthew 28:19, where are we to serve?

Does "all nations" mean just overseas?

Where could you start to be a missionary right now?

A NEW WAY TO BELIEVE

I recently heard a staggering statistic: The United States is the third-largest mission field in the world. Surprised? I was.

The church I worship at supports short-term missions trips to Honduras. Now isn't that more like it? Don't we generally think of missionaries as people who go overseas? After all, there is something appealing or exotic about traveling across oceans (to some of us anyway) to serve others.

Yet, the mission field actually is much larger right here in the United States, and there are actually Hondurans serving as missionaries in the United States. When I first read this, it seemed contrary to my traditional way of thinking.

What do you think? Do you think people in other countries need Jesus more than those in our own country?

Read the following list. Place a checkmark by each location you think may be a mission field for you:

__ Place of employment
__ School where you or a family member is a student
__ School where you can volunteer as a tutor
__ Doctor's office
__ Line at the grocery store
__ Habitat for Humanity building project
__ Orphanage overseas
__ Local YMCA
__ AIDS clinic in Africa
__ Community health clinic in your neighborhood
__ Your backyard
__ Your neighbor's backyard
__ Any place you can share God's love with others

What kinds of acts of service do missionaries engage in? Mark each you believe is a way missionaries serve:

__ Translating Bibles
__ Going with your friend to her doctor's appointment

___ Transporting elderly people to their medical appointments
___ Supervising your daughter's homework
___ Helping at an orphanage in Russia
___ Providing business training to single women in developing countries
___ Providing business training to budding entrepreneurs who just graduated from Harvard with an MBA
___ Teaching snowboarding
___ Helping college freshmen move into their dorm rooms
___ Any way you can share God's love with others

What does Ephesians 4:11-12 say to you?

Do you engage in Christian service? If so, in what way(s)?

Do these works of service need to be specifically volunteer or ministry activities, or can what you do during the day (parenting/profession/vocation/studying) be a ministry activity? How?

What does Colossians 3:23 say?

When my family participated in a missions trip to mainland Honduras, our daughters were involved in several different activities, including playing with the Honduran children while their families waited to be seen at the mobile medical clinic we set up in a rural one-room schoolhouse. They played ball, painted nails, braided hair, and drew pictures. On the days I helped mix cement by hand with sand collected from the riverbed, they removed rocks from the sand. They were missionaries, serving God in a way that fit their ages, talents, and abilities.

But they also serve locally, by helping with children's church, in the nursery, or with cleaning up after a fellowship meal.

May you do the same!

BELIEVE AND ACT

- Think of your workplace and home as your mission field.
- Encourage your entire family to view themselves as missionaries, calling them "God's representatives."
- Pick one new activity you can incorporate into your routine that is missional in nature, meaning it touches others with God's love.

ASK THROUGH PRAYER

Dear God,

Thank you for giving me special talents and abilities and my own unique personality. Please show me how I can use these to share your love with others through good words and good works.

Amen.

Day Five:

Actions Speak Louder Than Words

THOUGHT FOR THE DAY

Keep the words of St. Francis of Assisi in mind: "Share the gospel, use words if necessary." Service to the community, no strings attached, is a missional activity everyone can participate in.

WHAT DO YOU BELIEVE?

· Have you ever volunteered? Did you think of yourself as a missionary?
· Are there community service opportunities you can become involved in? If you do, will you think of yourself as a missionary?
· Is it okay to serve others if you expect something in return? For example, church attendance (but only if it is at your church).
· Have you witnessed churches effectively serving together in the community?

WHAT OTHERS MAY THINK

Outreach is:
a. Something only people who go into the Peace Corps do.

b. Volunteer work that sends me to the other side of town.
c. For young people-I'm too old and tired, and can't communicate with people different from me.
d. The local version of missions-simply sharing God's love in our community.

Let's keep building on this notion of missions. Hopefully you are becoming more comfortable with the idea that you can serve as a missionary. While my family has traveled to Honduras to serve, it is often more practical (and definitely less expensive) to start right where you are, in your home and neighborhood.

Outreach is the local version of missions work. After all, isn't it also part of The Great Commission? Doesn't "all nations" include your community as well as Honduras, China, Zimbabwe, or even Timbuktu?

There are plenty of people who engage in volunteer work-that's the "good works" part of the equation. What makes it outreach is serving with the motivation of sharing Christ's unconditional love with others.

Do you think it is necessary to be overt in your outreach efforts, stating that it is because of Christ and his sacrifice you are doing what you do? Or does it suffice to let your actions do the talking?

A friend recently commented to me, "If you need to ask me if I am a Christian, then I'm not doing a very good job of being Christ's ambassador." Do you agree with this statement? Why or why not?

Do you agree with these words of St. Francis of Assisi: "Share the gospel, use words if necessary"? Why or why not?

Do you think you need to earn the right to share with others why you value and treasure your relationship with Christ, or do you tell everyone you meet whether they want to hear it or not?

What motivates you to serve?

If someone asks you why you serve, what will you say? Can you explain the connection between service and your relationship with Jesus in a way that won't turn others off or demand they feel the same way?

What does it mean to you to love your neighbor?

As I get to know Jesus better and study his life and love, I value the opportunities I have to share that with others in the right way, time, and place. I would love for them to share in my experience. But what if they don't? Or choose to not come to church—especially my church—is that okay?

A NEW WAY TO BELIEVE

There is a saying, "People don't care how much you know until they know how much you care." Do you agree?

Can you think of a time in your life when someone genuinely showed you they cared? If so, how did you feel?

Were you more open to them as a result?

If you need a starting place, follow the advice in Hebrews 3:1: "So, my dear Christian friends, companions in following this call to the heights, *take a good hard look at Jesus. He's the centerpiece of everything we believe, faithful in everything God gave him to do*" (MSG, emphasis mine).

What does each of the following Scripture verses say about Jesus?

- Matthew 18:20
- John 8:36
- John 14:27
- 2 Corinthians 5:17
- Galatians 3:26
- Ephesians 2:14
- Ephesians 3:18
- Ephesians 5:2

· Philippians 4:13
· Colossians 3:13
· 2 Thessalonians 3:3
· 1 John 4:10

In your own words, write a description of Jesus and tell how you can model him to others through outreach:

Read Matthew 11:28. Whom does Jesus invite to follow him?

What two characteristics can we learn about Jesus in Matthew 11:29?

What does Matthew 11:29 tell us we will find for our souls?

One closing thought. Read Matthew 11:30. What does Jesus say about following him?

BELIEVE AND ACT
· Write the answers to the last four questions on an index card, and refer to it often as you seek to touch others through outreach for Christ.
· Add gentleness and humility to your service.
· If outreach becomes burdensome, ask Jesus to show you how you can rest.

ASK THROUGH PRAYER
Dear Jesus,

Thank you for being humble and gentle; this is so refreshing in the chaos of the world we live in. Help me show others through outreach that by knowing and following you, they too can add the simplicity of your example to their lives.

Amen.

Let's Get Personal: From Rules to Relationships

The running joke in our family about wedding attendance revolves around placing bets on whether we will walk down the aisle before or after the bride. I half think it's some sort of passive-aggressive tendency we have developed because every church has its own way of doing things and we never seem quite sure when to sit, stand, or kneel. We spend the entire service glancing sideways to take cues from the people sitting around us. We just hope they know what they're doing. There just seem to be so many rules.

My first real exposure to faith was through a friend's faith. In my earliest days of Bible study, I never knew the difference between the Old and the New Testaments, an epistle or an apostle, or who Christ was. There was never any mention of the Holy Spirit or Satan, but plenty of attention to how I should behave and what I should wear. Appear in church in blue jeans? I might be asked to leave.

I also had a confusing experience with the faith my husband was raised in before we got married. My husband was brought up in a very strict religion, and his family wanted to share their faith with me. I know they really, really hoped I would accept their beliefs and that maybe my husband would jump on board, too, something he hadn't done up to that point despite being brought up going to church every Sunday and Bible

School every summer, and hearing his father say basically the same prayer before every meal his entire life.

I was given a Bible and we were on our way to becoming a "good Christian couple." But I did not choose to become a part of their tradition because I never experienced those things I needed the most: grace, which embodied understanding, forgiveness, and loving me just the way I was. I felt expected to dress a certain way, couldn't pray, and somehow felt like I never quite measured up. The Bible I received was full of language I didn't understand (lots of thee's and thou's) and the jewelry I loved to wear was a bit on the flashy side.

When we went to church I was uncomfortable and bored. The group seemed closed and I didn't feel like I fit in. I felt bad enough about myself; I didn't need God peering down at me from the Pearly Gates shaking his head and scrutinizing my every move, letting me know subtly and not so subtly I just didn't measure up. I was good enough at doing that myself. I agreed with my husband's "thanks but no thanks" response to his family's religion.

What I needed was faith in Jesus, the Lover of my soul, which involved forgiveness, love, and grace. I finally found it several years later in the loving arms of Christ. How wonderful it was to be involved in a relationship rather than a regimen!

Day One:

You Mean I Really Do Get to Start Over?

THOUGHT FOR THE DAY

No matter what mistakes you have made in your life, God desires a personal (not distant or ritualistic) relationship with you.

WHAT DO YOU BELIEVE?

· Does each day really bring a new beginning?
· Does God expect us to engage in rigid, ritualistic behavior to approach him?
· What if I really, really mess up-does that make a difference? Will God still love me?
· Is it ever too late to start over?

WHAT OTHERS MAY THINK

New Creation is:
a. What my lemon meringue pies are.
b. My daughter's kindergarten art.
c. My house after major, major cleaning.
d. Your life in Christ after you have surrendered it to him.

We've already talked about U-turns. Now let's take it a step further. Not just a U-turn but a journey in a new direction.

Not too long after I made a commitment to follow Christ (which might have also been labeled by others as "being saved," "accepting Christ," "becoming a Christian," "coming to faith," or probably a bazillion other labels that don't really offer a totally satisfactory definition), my husband told me, "Kathy, I really like the person you are becoming."

I glanced over at him as a smile spread across my face.

Then he paused, turned ten shades of red, and stammered, "Uh, uh, I-I-I don't mean it how it sounds" and continued to try to dig himself out of the hole he perceived himself to be in.

But to my ears he couldn't have said anything nicer, because it meant there were noticeable changes in my persona. Dramatic changes; positive changes.

And I told him his words were perfect and I appreciated the compliment.

Can you think of people who accepted Christ and over time changed for the better?

Do you think that sometimes people who accepted Christ as a child because it was expected, or assumed faith because it was what their parents believed, need to make a re-commitment or renewal of faith to make it their own?

(Please note that I am NOT saying their commitment isn't recognized by God. For their faith to be lived out in a relevant way, however, it may be helpful to consciously make the commitment again at an age when they have more of an understanding of what they are committing to.)

How do you perceive God? Do you think of him as a:

a. Disinterested mega-spirit who just kind of hangs out?
b. Punitive "can't wait to catch you" mistake-zapper who sounds like the great wizard of Oz?

c. Grand, vague, and disinterested spirit who you know in theory loves you, but with whom a personal relationship is impossible.

d. A caring, loving parent who yearns to get to know you personally and delights in you. At the same time he is also disappointed when you make mistakes and yearns to be consulted as you live your life.

How do you think you came to that impression of God?

Who were the influential people in your life who helped shape your impression of God?

If you always thought of God as angry or distant, how do you feel about getting to know Jesus, who personifies God in humility, grace, forgiveness, and acceptance?

It was a long time before I really realized the difference between: (1) the Old Covenant between God and his people, and (2) the New Covenant. So here is a very, very basic synopsis:

The Old Covenant, the promise between God and his chosen people, the Israelites, is recorded in the Ten Commandments, and can be read in Exodus 20:1-17. It included many laws and regulations.

Animal sacrifice was required to be right with God. The priests were the only ones allowed in the Holy Place in the tabernacle (and later the temple), and only one time each year could the high priest enter into the Most Holy Place, inside which resided the Ark of the Covenant. By Jesus' time, super-religious groups like the Pharisees and Sadducees controlled Judaism in Jerusalem. They had added tons of rules, making holy living (or their version of it, at least) virtually impossible.

The New Covenant came to pass when God sent his Son, Jesus, to Earth to live among people. I know it's kind of hard to grasp but Jesus was completely God and completely man. (Jesus is referred to as both Son of God and Son of Man.) He became the once-and-for-all, final sacrifice through the shedding of his blood on the cross for all of humanity's sins, so that whoever professes faith in him is redeemed and made right with God.

It is a covenant (promise) made by God based wholly on his gift of grace and mercy to us as a result of our faith and belief in Jesus. (That's why Jesus is also called Messiah, Savior, Christ, Redeemer—all of which mean someone who saves us from our sins.) Love is the primary ingredient. Love God and love your neighbor—that's it for the rules.

Okay, so we have Jesus, and we have the Pharisees. The following verses from Matthew 15 paint an accurate picture of the Pharisees and how they related to Christ.

· What are the Pharisees concerned about in verse 2?

· How does Jesus refer to them in verse 7?

· In verse 8, how does he say the Pharisees worship him?

· Is their worship worthwhile? Why not (verse 9)?

· Now read Hebrews 10:8-10. Which covenant does this describe?

· What kinds of offerings were described in verse 8?

· Did they please God? If not, why were they performed?

· What is the purpose of the New Covenant (verse 9)?

· How have we been made holy (verse 10)?

· Is this a one-time event, or do we need to go back again and again?

· According to Hebrews 10:16, how will we know God's laws?

A NEW WAY TO BELIEVE

When we cross the faith threshold and the New Covenant applies to us, we are actually adopted into God's family. That's why we end up with so many brothers and sisters!

What does Ephesians 1:5 tell us?

How are we described in 2 Corinthians 5:17?

Read Galatians 5:16. How are we instructed to live after we have become a part of God's family?

Galatians 5:19 lists the attributes of the sinful nature. Even though we discussed these in Chapter 4, it doesn't hurt to review them, so re-read the verse. How have we been given new life?

Read Ephesians 2:8. Does salvation have anything to do with what we do, or is it a gift?

What are we taught to do in Ephesians 4:22?

How will we be made new (verse 23)?

In verse 24, what are we instructed to put on? How are we to be?

BELIEVE AND ACT

- When we are "born again" we start our new lives and, over time, change to become more Christlike. This transformation occurs with the help of the Holy Spirit.

· It is a privilege and responsibility to be part of God's family.
· God has special jobs and a purpose for us to fulfill here on Earth.

ASK THROUGH PRAYER

Lord,

Thank you so, so much for the gift of new life in you. Thank you also for your Spirit, the Holy Spirit, whom you have sent to be my guide. Thank you for lending meaning to my life.

Amen.

Day Two:

If You Open the Closet Door, the Skeletons May Fall Out

THOUGHT FOR THE DAY
Sin refers to our separation from God, which results from poor choices we have made-nothing more, nothing less.

WHAT DO YOU BELIEVE?
· Is one sin worse than another?
· Do you think of yourself as a sinner?
· Have you heard sin described as separation from God?

WHAT OTHERS MAY THINK
Sin is:
a. Heinous acts that land people in jail.
b. An out-of-date way of saying something is "too bad."
c. Something only really, really bad people do.
d. Anything that is displeasing to God and causes separation from him.

Let's face it—most of us don't like the word sin. It's just too strong. Sin is something reserved for those really, really bad people, but certainly not me.

After all, I only tell a "white lie" or "stretch the truth" a little bit (or sneak candy into the movie theater because they charge too much for it and I've already paid an arm and a leg to get in).

It's simply much easier to rationalize our choices and behavior, explaining away the small inconveniences or interpretations of truth. There is no black and white except in extreme situations, and we live our lives according to a palette of multiple shades of gray.

How does Webster's define sin?

How do you define sin?

Is sinner a word you would ever use to describe yourself? Why or why not?

How many of the Ten Commandments can you list? (If you're stumped, refer to Exodus 20:1-17.)

Most of us would view murder and adultery as sins. But what about if you think someone "got what they deserved"—someone's death, or an affair with someone's spouse? Is murder or adultery ever justified?

What about stealing? Have you ever stolen anything? Which of the following do you consider stealing?

___ Taking a soda refill even though you know they aren't free
___ Passing off your child as young enough for the child admission price, even when his birthday was seven months ago and he's now considered an adult

___ Shoplifting
___ Accepting donations to support a service project after the money has already been turned in
___ Making copies of a music CD you bought for your friends so they wouldn't need to purchase their own.

Okay, now here's one I have a hard time with. "Thou shalt not covet thy neighbour's house . . . nor anything that is thy neighbour's" (Exodus 20:17 KJV). Uh-oh . . . I'm done.

I live in a lovely home in a development with gorgeous views in the rolling hills of central Pennsylvania. We were one of the first families to build in this development. Our house is large, but not superficially ornate.

As more homes were added to the development, they got bigger and bigger, laminate and Corian countertops were replaced with granite, colonial homes were surpassed by sprawling residences, and basements were being finished at a cost easily higher than the median home prices in some communities.

I would be lying if I said I wasn't envious (or covetous) of different features some of my neighbor's homes boasted.

Not to mention cars (a new minivan complete with DVD player); a screened-in porch (always thought one of those would be nice); new patio furniture (ours is rusty); or the beautiful water garden complete with waterfall (how relaxing).

And the list could go on and on: jewelry, clothing, scrapbooking supplies, furniture, kid's clothing . . . Anytime I have a "green attack" (green with envy) I am falling into the envy trap which can be a slippery slope.

Are there things you are covetous of?

Do you want these things more than you want an intimate relationship with God?

Do you spend more time shopping than you do getting to know God better?

Does the thought of a good sale excite you more than going to church on Sunday morning?

Do you think that if you put material possessions ahead of spending time with God that puts you in the position of making idols for yourself?

What about the commandment "You shall have no other gods before me"? Do you think those "gods" could be anything you are more devoted to than you are to the true God? What about work? School? Even family?

What about the New Covenant? What if you don't love your neighbor as yourself? Is that sin?

Does it matter if you are separated from God? Why or why not?

A NEW WAY TO BELIEVE
What does Romans 3:23 say?

What does Galatians 3:4 say? Do you think that applies to you also? Are you part of the "all" God refers to?

How uncomfortable is it to think of yourself as a sinner? Are there other, more palatable words?

How seriously do you think God views our sins, or mistakes?

What matters to God (1 Corinthians 7:19)?

How seriously should we take our sin?

What can we do to make ourselves right with God?

What does God's Word say in Jeremiah 16:19?

How does Webster's define repent?

Have you ever thought of repentance as "refreshing?" Read Acts 3:19; what does it say to you?

What do you think "refreshing" means in this context?

Is repentance simply saying you're sorry, or is it accompanied by other emotions?

Can God recognize anguish and sorrow?

What does Luke 13:3 say?

Who did Jesus come to call (Luke 5:32)?

If there are things you have done, or thought, or said in your life that you need to repent of, take a moment now to do so in prayer to God.

Read John 1:29. Who does John the Baptist say takes away the sin of the world?

Would you want someone to tell you if they noticed you doing something wrong if it helped you become a better person and more Christ-like? If we notice someone else caught in sin, what should we do (Galatians 6:1)?

How should we speak to them (Ephesians 4:15)?

BELIEVE AND ACT
· By virtue of the fact that we are human, we will make mistakes and do things displeasing to God. As soon as you realize that this is the case, take a moment to offer God your repentance.
· Help be a guide and teacher to others along the journey in a way that is loving and supportive and serves to make you a good representative of Christ.
· Ask God to reveal thoughts and behaviors that are shades of gray in your mind but that are black to him.

ASK THROUGH PRAYER
Dear God,

Even though I don't like the word sinner and don't like to think of myself as one, help me realize there are things I do on a daily basis that displease you. Help me to experience your love and grace and recognize how to live my life in a way that represents your heart and your kingdom here on Earth.

Amen.

DAY THREE:

ALL ARE WELCOME, AND You CAN EVEN WEAR JEANS

THOUGHT FOR THE DAY

It doesn't matter what we wear to church. What matters is the condition of our hearts.

WHAT DO YOU BELIEVE?
- Can a person be a Christian and sip on a glass of wine?
- Do you think you need to dress a certain way to go to church?
- Can someone with multiple body piercings and tattoos be a Christian?
- How would you feel if a homeless person sat next to you in church?
- Can a person be gay and be a Christian?

WHAT OTHERS MAY THINK
Appearance is:
  a. How we prove to others we have it all together.
  b. What celebrities, even church celebrities, make when they speak at big meetings.

    c. What teenagers grace us with for five minutes twice a week at the dinner table.

    d. What outwardly doesn't matter to God; he cares much more about your heart than your outward appearance.

Occasionally I glance in the mirror and point to my nose. Right there, I think as I tilt my head to the side and point to the dip just above my nostril—a small diamond stud. In fact, I have had several people tell me they think a small nose ring would be quite attractive. I think so, too.

I also think a small tattoo representing my faith in Christ would be kind of cool. I would put it in an unobtrusive place on my lower back where I have plenty of padding and it wouldn't be quite so painful.

The reason I probably won't follow through isn't because the Bible forbids it (because that would be a reason to not do it) but rather because I think I'm too old for a nose ring and too chicken for a tattoo (besides which my husband is a dermatologist and takes them off as part of his professional duties).

As a Christian I have a responsibility to help fellow Christians be accountable for their behavior, love, and service to Christ; but my approach with people who are not yet in God's family is different. When I approach people who are not yet a part of the church (God's family) I need to go slow and leave the judgment up to God. My goal should be to share Jesus in a loving way, rather than wagging my finger at them and peering down at them in a condemning way, perhaps with a bit of shame thrown in for good measure. It is not my job to scrutinize and judge.

I love what Dan Kimball writes in his book *They Like Jesus but Not the Church*. He writes, "We should be careful not to make judgments based on personal opinions rather than on the clear teaching of Scripture." He continues, "I have talked to many wounded younger Christians who left the church because they were confronted in a legalistic way about extra-biblical things."

Read 1 Samuel 16:7. What does it say?

Read Galatians 2:6. What does it say?

Why do you think this message would be given by God in both the Old and New Testaments?

Have you ever felt judged because of how you looked? This can refer to clothing, jewelry, tattoos, or any other aspect of your appearance.

On the flip side, have there been times you have been embraced by others who are Christians and it didn't seem to matter to them how you looked?

What about modesty? Do you think it is important to dress modestly? Why or why not?

Do you think the outward appearance matters to God when we worship him? Why or why not?

A NEW WAY TO BELIEVE

Wearing your Sunday best . . . it's an idea I can't completely shake. I remember when I went to church with my great-grandmother as a child. I always wore my best dress, whitest socks with lace trim, and shiniest shoes. As I got older I still dressed up when I went to church. But I didn't feel so beautiful inside, and wasn't that what was important to God, the condition of my heart?

I have come to accept and realize that I had it backwards all those years. I was gussying up on the outside, but inside I was a mess. I stayed angry at people, wanted my own way, and was generally pretty self-absorbed.

The thought of going to church in blue jeans shocked me. Yet why should it? Far better to be somewhat less color-coordinated on the outside, but pure of heart on the inside.

I love it when my sister-in-law comes to worship with me. But she, like many other people I know, can't get past getting all dressed up for church. She feels that somehow God can't accept her worship if she isn't all dolled up. I find it much more freeing to know that God looks at the motives of my heart rather than my outward appearance.

But what often happens is I DO take care in making myself look special for worship because in a sense I am going on a date with Jesus, and since he is so special to me I WANT to look my best.

Would you feel less intimidated about attending church if you knew there wasn't a "dress code" and you could truly "come as you are" and be free to worship?

Have you ever worshipped at a church such as that?

What about Bible Study, or small groups? Do you feel the same need or expectation to dress a certain way to attend worship in those settings?

Read 1 Timothy 2:9. How do you interpret "dress modestly"? What about "with decency and propriety, not with braided hair or gold or pearls or expensive clothes?"

Do you think the image of attire is different depending on the culture and historical time frame?

What would modest dress in the United States look like? Would it differ by region?

If anything, it seems as if we are urged to stay away from showy dress and "Sunday best" if it involves expensive clothes and lots of jewelry. Do you think that still applies today as much as it did almost 2,000 years ago?

Is it as fair to search the person's heart to ensure it is pure in cases where they do dress to the nines?

Read Psalm 139:23. Whom do we want God to search? And what are we asking that He know about?

Do you think God can search us and know our heart equally well if we are fresh home from work, in blue jeans, or in our Sunday best?

Based on your answers, what are you more likely to pay attention to the next time you worship? What you wear, or what is deep inside your heart?

BELIEVE AND ACT

· The next time you go to church, pay closer attention to preparing your heart than your hair.
· Go with an attitude of worship, regardless of what you are wearing.
· Encourage others who may be more preoccupied with how they look than how they act to remember that God cares more about the condition of their heart.

ASK THROUGH PRAYER

Lord,

Help me pay special attention to how I look to you and not to others. Help me have a heart makeover if that is what I need. The only one I want to impress is you, not those around me. Thank you.

Amen.

DAY FOUR:

WOULD YOU STILL LOVE ME IF YOU REALLY KNEW ME?

THOUGHT FOR THE DAY

Many of us have had difficulties in our lives and have made mistakes. Jim Cymbala, in his book *Fresh Power*, writes about David Berkowitz, the "Son of Sam" murderer, and the forgiveness and love he has received from God and others. What is your reaction to such radical forgiveness?

WHAT DO YOU BELIEVE?

· Are you willing to transparently share with others mistakes you have made?

· Have you been judged or shunned by others when you have shared about your shortcomings?

· Do you feel there are mistakes you have made that God can't forgive?

· Do you think it is harder to forgive yourself than for God to forgive you?

WHAT OTHERS MAY THINK

Forgiveness is:

a. What you flippantly say you will give, but then continue to hold a grudge.

b. What you beg for from offended parties when you know you have made a mistake.
c. What bitter people can't give.
d. The ultimate act of extending God's love to others.

Forgiveness is a Biblical biggie. It is one of those major pillars of the Christian faith and gets plenty of attention throughout the Bible. Clearly God has several lessons he yearns for us to learn, but unfortunately many of us are slow learners (myself included).

In addition to stressing the central message of forgiveness, God also pays close attention to the condition of our hearts. And I believe that the ability to forgive and the condition of our hearts are closely interwoven.

Thank God he gives us plenty of examples on what this looks like, how to do it, why to do it, and a general all-purpose blueprint for living a life that ends up emulating Christ. In fact, Christ's last request was an appeal made to God to forgive those who were about to crucify him (Luke 23:34).

We have a friend who lost a brother in an accident involving a car and a motorcycle. The driver of the car was young and reckless; alcohol had been involved. Yet the victim's family held deep faith convictions and chose to forgive, not "sticking it to him" in court. They had the power to ensure that this young man "paid" for what he did for the rest of his life. Yet they chose to forgive him, because to them that is what their faith mandated.

"How can we not forgive him, when daily God forgives us for the mistakes we make?"

My friend paused, contemplating and remembering the devastating loss of his brother.

"It doesn't make it easy, and we will never forget, but through God's strength and grace, he enabled us to forgive so another life wasn't lost."

This experience had a profound effect on me. Could I do the same in the same situation?

I contrast this story with that of a young man involved in an automobile accident that also resulted in a fatality. Alcohol had been consumed earlier in the day, and a child lost her life.

The outcome has been very different. Forgiveness was not part of the equation. But a calculated approach that included vendetta ("We'll get you if it's the last thing we do") and political agenda was part of this story. The district attorney prosecuting the case was running for judge and this would be his landmark case.

The DA was successful in securing a verdict of guilty on charges of second degree murder, and the man in question was sentenced to twenty-two years to life in prison. I agree there needed to be punishment and consequence, but I also believe his consequence (sentence) was too harsh. He has served 22 years of his sentence and has children who are growing up without a father. He will come up for parole in two years. What difference would forgiveness make in this situation?

Are there situations you are holding on to in which it is hard or seemingly impossible for you to forgive?

What do you think the outcome would be if you forgave?

How do you think you would change as a result of this choice?

Are there times you really believe you have forgiven someone, only to learn there are still times when unforgiveness manifests itself?

What are some of the ways this can happen?

Do you think forgiveness is more for the person being forgiven or for the person doing the forgiving?

What are some of the things that prevent you from forgiving others?

Do you think it is ever too late to forgive someone for a transgression?

Do you think it is possible to forgive someone for a past transgression if they are no longer alive? If so, how could you do this?

A NEW WAY TO BELIEVE

Through his words and his life, Jesus gives us lots of direction and insight into forgiveness. The hard part is the same in this case as it is with most of the lessons God has for us. Because he has given us a mind of our own (often referred to as "free will") we have a choice as to whether we choose to follow through with his example or directive.

There are several attitudes that interfere with our ability to obey God, and because God made us, he recognizes what they are. They include pride (not being able to humble ourselves and recognize God's way as better); stubbornness (wanting to do things our way); hard-heartedness (thinking we have a better handle on the big picture), and greed (if there's something in it for me, go for it).

Read Matthew 6:12. Most of us, even if we haven't graced a church in years are familiar with this verse, taken from the Lord's Prayer. But how many of us really think about what it says? "Forgive us our debts as we also have forgiven our debtors." What strikes you about this verse and its message about forgiveness?

Do you tend to stop applying the message in this verse after the first part of the request/statement? In other words, do you readily accept the part about asking God to forgive our trespasses, but not apply the second part of the verse, which explicitly states that we will be forgiven to the extent we forgive others?

Based on how forgiving you are in general, this could be great news, or pretty bad news.

I guess Jesus thought we might have difficulty with this verse, as he adds just a bit more clarification at the end of Matthew 6. What does Jesus say in verses 14 and 15?

How forgiving do you consider yourself to be?

__ So forgiving I let myself get walked all over.
__ A little bit forgiving, but it's hard for me. I tend to hold
   on to things.
__ I can forgive the small stuff, but not the big stuff.
__ I am pretty easygoing and, over time, able to forgive most
   things.
__ I take seriously the mandate to forgive others the way
   God has forgiven me, and know God will give me
   strength to do this when it is otherwise just impossible.

God also indicates it is never too late to seek reconciliation and it is even more important than presenting our gifts to God at the altar. What does Matthew 5:23-24 say?

Is it good enough to forgive just once, or even a couple of times? What does Matthew 18:21-22 say? Do you think you have the capacity to forgive that much?

Jesus tells a story in Matthew 18:23-35 to illustrate this point. The end of the story, as told in *The Message*, states, "That's exactly what my Father in heaven is going to do to each one of you who doesn't forgive unconditionally anyone who asks for mercy"—he will put the screws to you.

If we aren't initially motivated out of love, maybe fear (or a healthy respect for God's consequences) will help us get to that place.

Do you agree with the statement, "Forgiveness is the salve that when applied to the wounds of hurt and bitterness helps to promote healing"? Is there someone you need to forgive?

If there is someone you feel owes you an apology, can you take the first step toward reconciliation? Why or why not?

What other insight can we gain from Ephesians 4:31-32 to avoid problems, thus negating the need for forgiveness and reconciliation?

Who is the final authority on forgiveness (Ephesians 4:32)?

BELIEVE AND ACT
· Make it a point to get rid of bitterness. Your entire life will become sweeter. If you season your interactions with humility, bitterness will fade.
· If you are on poor terms with someone, take the first step toward reconciliation, forgiveness, and healing.
· Develop an attitude of gratitude for all the grace and forgiveness God extends to you and seek to be a conduit of that toward others.

ASK THROUGH PRAYER
Our Father in heaven,
Reveal who you are.
Set the world right;
Do what's best—as above, so below.
Keep us alive with three square meals.
Keep us forgiven with you and forgiving others.
Keep us safe from ourselves and the Devil.
You're in charge!
You can do anything you want!
You're ablaze in beauty!
Yes. Yes. Yes. (Matthew 6:9-13 MSG)
Amen.

Day Five:

I'd Like You to Meet My Best Friend

THOUGHT FOR THE DAY

Is it difficult to think of Jesus as your best friend? Can you imagine describing your friendship with Jesus the same way you would describe your friendship with your best friend or husband?

WHAT DO YOU BELIEVE?
- How often do you hear other people talk about Jesus as their best friend?
- When others share Jesus with you, do you feel as if they are introducing their best friend?
- Do you think of Jesus as a new friend?

WHAT OTHERS MAY THINK
Jesus is:
a. A word you hear used as an exclamatory profanity.
b. A fictional character.
c. One of the world's great prophets and/or teachers.
d. The living Lord and Savior and sole Way to everlasting life.

Explain your answer:

· How does Jesus describe himself in John 14:6?

· What does this mean to you?

· Have others introduced Jesus to you as the one true God?

· What has their approach been?

· Have you shared Jesus using the above passage? Were you able to respond to questions about why you believe what you believe?

According to 1 Peter 3:15, how are we to do this? When are we supposed to be prepared to do this?

Have you or others you know been successful in sharing according to the Biblical mandate given in this passage?

The following passage is excerpted from Dan Kimball's *They Like Jesus but Not the Church*:

> We need to be wise missionaries, taking into considera-tion the culture people of emerging generations are being raised in and how they think . . . In my conversations with people outside the faith, I have been able to strongly and clearly explain to them the exclusive claims of Jesus and my belief that salvation comes through Jesus alone. I don't have to hide anything or water anything down because my approach makes all the difference. Because I

have established relationships with them, listened to their spiritual perspectives, and built trust with them, I have been able to share Jesus' words that he is the way, the truth, and the life and that no one comes to the Father but through him. I have found that people are actually curious about Jesus' statement, and I've had positive dialogue with them about it . . . But before we can have such conversations with people, we have to build relationships with them and understand other faiths well enough that we can talk about them intelligently.

Do you agree or disagree? In what way(s)?

Does the passage above have any impact on how you might share Jesus with others?

Is this passage in sync with 1 Peter 3:15?

A NEW WAY TO BELIEVE

When I was a kid in the early '70s, there was a show on TV called *The Courtship of Eddie's Father.* (I bet now it's on Nick at Night.)

The theme song started out with the words, "People let me tell you about my best friend . . ."

What qualities does your best friend have?

Who is number one in your life? Is it your spouse, your child, your parent? Or is it Jesus?

Not long after I had made my commitment to follow Christ, I remember hearing a relatively newlywed Christian couple tell each other in conversation, "I love you number two." I didn't get it and they didn't explain.

Then a few weeks later it hit me. They were referring to loving each other second after Jesus. I was so excited by this moment of epiphany that I got on the phone and interrupted the wife at work. When she answered the phone, I practically shrieked at her, "I get it, I get it! Remember when you told Dave, 'I love you number two?' Well, I finally get it!"

I imagine she thought I was nuts. But to recognize Jesus as number one in my life and my best friend, who knows me intimately inside and out, puts my well-being first, is the Lover of my soul, and wants me to experience the splendor of life with him, not only today but forever, was a huge revelation for me.

Jesus is the Lover of your soul and wants to get to know you as his best friend.

His love endures forever (2 Corinthians 5:13); is unfailing (Psalm 33:18); is abounding (Psalm 103:8); is priceless (Psalm 36:7); is great (Psalm 57:10); is better than life (Psalm 63:3); is slow to anger (Psalm 145:8); covers all wrongs (Proverbs 10:12); is as strong as death (Song of Solomon 8:6); is faithful (Isaiah 55:3); is everlasting (Jeremiah 31:3); is comforting (Zephaniah 3:17); is great (John 15:13); is patient and kind, does not delight in evil, and never fails (1 Corinthians 13:4, 6, 8); and is available to each one of us.

The invitation is there: "Are you tired? Worn out? Burned out on religion? Come to me. Get away with me and you'll recover your life. I'll show you how to take a real rest. Walk with me and work with me-watch how I do it. Learn the unforced rhythms of grace. I won't lay anything heavy or ill-fitting on you. Keep company with me and you'll learn to live freely and lightly" (Matthew 11:28 MSG).

BELIEVE AND ACT

- If you don't have a personal friendship with Jesus, the door is always open for you to enter into it at any time.
- Jesus doesn't love according to human standards; his love is unfailing and will never let you down.
- Remember that by modeling Christ's love to others, you can introduce many new friends to him.

ASK THROUGH PRAYER

Dear Jesus,

Thank you for being my friend, whether or not I am a friend to you in return. Thank you for wanting to be everyone's friend. Thank you for letting me be a friend to others on your behalf. Please deepen my friendship with you so, even though you know everything about me, I still can't wait to run to you with my delights and despairs. I love you, and thank you for loving me.

Amen.

CONCLUSION

If we were sitting at a coffee house, or somewhere else enjoying some food and drink, I would want to continue the conversation and pick your brain. I would want to hear your thoughts in response to the questions asked in the What do You Believe section and also the responses in the What do You Think section.

What is your take? Are Christians loving or judgmental? Or most likely both, since we are all only human... Do you know more people who are not Christians who live truer to the golden rule than self identified Christians? Transparency in admitting where human beings have let each other down is necessary, and a little bit of humor doesn't hurt.

My prayer is that this study will give you some hope that pop culture or popular perception are very different from the Biblical way of defining certain words and that a bridge of understanding a little more about Jesus, the church and Christians would be built.

Jesus came to heal, not condemn.

Feel free to drop me an email: Kathy@Kathypride.com. I look forward to continuing the conversation.